More
Theatre
Games

**Improvisations
and exercises
for developing
acting skills**

for
Young
Performers

Suzi Zimmerman

MERIWETHER PUBLISHING LTD.
Colorado Springs, Colorado

Meriwether Publishing Ltd., Publisher
PO Box 7710
Colorado Springs, CO 80933-7710

Executive editor: Arthur L. Zapel
Assistant editor: Dianne Bundt
Cover design: Jan Melvin

Library of Congress Cataloging-in-Publication Data

Zimmerman, Suzi.
    More theatre games for young performers : improvisations and exercises for developing acting skills / Suzi Zimmerman. -- 1st ed.
        p. cm.
    Includes bibliographical references and index.
    ISBN 1-56608-096-7 (trade pbk.)
1. Improvistion (Acting) 2. Acting. 3. Drama in education. I. Title.
    PN2071.I5Z56 2004
    792.02'8--dc22

                            2004005159

        1   2   3   04   05   06

There was speech in their dumbness, language in their very gesture.

— William Shakespeare, The Winter's Tale, Act V, Scene ii

Special thanks to ...

The many people who generously allowed me to use
their stories, games, pictures, and ideas in this book,

The students and teachers who donated
additional activities and posed for pictures,

My agent, who stood by me when I refused to audition
because I had to work on this project,

My friends, whom I haven't seen in ages
because I had to work on this project,
(I am almost done — *promise!*)

My children, who (again) ate pizza and leftovers
because I had to work on this project,

And especially to ...
My husband, who never questioned my labor of love,
and who encourages me in *all* that I do.

Contents

Chapter 5
Games 108

Chapter 6
Improvisation 132

Chapter 7
Pantomime

Chapter 8
Nonacting Theatre Games and Activities

Introduction

Remember when you were a kid, sitting in class listening to the teacher talk about this or that, her voice a little too monotone to maintain your interest? In the meantime, you entertained yourself by watching the hands on the clock slowly tick their way around the face. They seemed to tease the students with their rhythmic clicking dance, and at one point seemed to stop altogether for a hearty yawn and a taunting stretch. Or maybe you were one of the lucky students whose creative teacher broke the monotony of the daily lecture by showing a movie, and again, the hypnotic click, click, click of the filmstrip put you to sleep.

Some classes require that students sit in their desks each day and endure countless hours of lecturing and listening, but not the drama class. Some classes have so much data that taking notes from start to finish is — well, is almost imperative, but not the drama class. And some classes need the structure and quiet of a well-managed library, but not the drama class. The truth is, in middle and high school, there are very few lessons in theatre that require students to take notes at great length. Even those that do require the onset of writers' cramp can benefit from a balance of both intellect and action. Even at the more intense college level, good instructors recognize the necessity of creativity and action in lessons.

At some point in history, an actor — or perhaps a director — made a comparison between what children thought was fun and what actors do on stage. He must have realized that the more fun the actors were having, the more energy they seemed to have for their acting. Thus, the recipe for successfully training actors with games and fun activities was likely born. After all, what do we call that thing we perform? Oh, yes. A play.

As children, we play dress up, we sneak into our mothers' makeup drawers and draw grotesquely beautiful smiles on our faces, and we act like grownups. Later in life we begin hearing phrases like "Act your age" and "Grow up." So we do, and when we do, we forget the one element that makes learning stick. We forget to have fun. The newly born "grownup" does not see this as a handicap, for everyone else is acting grownup, too.

Then, one day you see a play performance. The actors are running up and down the stairs, in one door, out the next, speaking in wonderful

British accents. The play is *Noises Off* by Michael Frayn, and the title fits. For a short while, you forget you are watching a performance and get caught up in the antics. You laugh until your side hurts, and when the curtain comes down at the end, you clap heartily and think to yourself, "Well, that looked like fun. I wish I could be an actor." And as you leave the theatre, you have an energetic bounce in your step that was not there before.

The Top Ten Reasons to Use Theatre Games in Your Program:
   10. You or your students are burned out and need to refuel
   9. Your class or cast is in a rut, no longer taking risks, stuck on a boring plane; you need a way to tap into their creativity again
   8. You have a new skill you want to teach them and a game would either teach the skill or serve as a transition to the new lesson
   7. The students have just learned a new skill, and now they need a way to practice it without taking the time to find, memorize, and rehearse a scene
   6. Students are timid, shy, self-conscious; if you don't loosen them up a little, they will never feel free to explore characterization, movement, expression, levels, intensity, and voice
   5. Students have worked hard on a production, studying for a test, or on scenes, and they deserve a day of no-holds-barred FUN!
   4. One class is getting ahead of the others and needs a way to slow down while waiting for the others to catch up
   3. A number of students are absent, and to proceed with the lesson would leave them behind and cause a lengthy repetition of the same material upon their return
   2. There are only a few minutes of class remaining — too little to begin a new lesson and too much for free time
   And the Number 1 reason to use theatre games and other fun activities in class is ...
   You are being observed by your principal or educational evaluator and need a fun, energetic, hands-on activity that will impress even the stuffiest red pen and make you look an awful lot like the next "Teacher of the Year!" (So don't forget to use the discussion circle followed by a *Game Evaluation*.)

Many different types of people are drawn to the theatre for a countless number of reasons. Shy people act because they can boldly become the bad guy, the vixen, or the evil stepmother. Funny people act because they can get away with acting silly, being devilish, or playing tricks on others without someone telling them to "grow up." Those with handicaps act because there is a place for everyone on stage, and production casts are like warm, safe, tight-knit families. The class clown with too much energy acts because on stage there is rarely such a thing as "too much energy," and his director will appreciate him. And the angry kid — you know, the one with the big chip on his shoulder — acts because the stage offers him a kind of therapy that even the best money cannot buy. Even the most grounded, level-headed, normal people act because it's challenging, rewarding, and most of all — FUN!

Yes, acting is fun. It is energetic, and dynamic. It really is not conducive to a typical classroom filled with desks and chairs, nor will a truly active drama class fit well in the same hall as the quiet school library. Your average, everyday lecturer cannot teach theatre any more than a band teacher could teach a student to play without having a musical instrument in his hands. Granted, there are a number of facts that students of the stage must learn, so I cannot condone never taking notes. What I am saying is that every note should be balanced with a little lab work — some hands-on learning.

According to Bloom's Taxonomy, the most basic levels of learning are knowledge and comprehension. This means students can remember and understand the information the teacher is relaying. These are basically the only two levels of learning that are being exercised when students take notes and then take a test. The higher levels of learning include application, analysis, synthesis, and evaluation; in other words, students can use the knowledge (apply it), break it down into parts (analyze it) and also build from it (use it to synthesize a new whole), and lastly, they can assess its value (evaluate it). It is our job as teachers to ensure that these loftier levels of learning are taking place in our classrooms. It means our jobs will be more difficult and our creativity will be working overtime, but the rewards will be priceless.

Take theatre history, for example. It was the one unit I dreaded as a student because I knew we would have to take notes from bell to bell. Oh, and there was always that big test at the end, too. How could a teacher possibly make that fun and offer the kids some hands-on learning? Scene work and improvisation are just a couple of ways, and there are always research projects, videos, demonstrations, and more.

For the sake of this book, however, let's talk about just the gaming end of the spectrum. Later in this book, you will read about an activity called *Not Just Another Board Game,* that will help you teach theatre history. The students will create a life-sized board game using materials that can be found on most campuses. Not only will they learn the facts of theatre history, you can set up your game so that they actually move through "time." You can increase the level of learning by having them take on characters, learn lines from plays, and even have cards that require them to act out scenes. In the end, they will have learned the same facts they would have using traditional note taking, plus they will have also taken advantage of their intrinsic creativity and higher thinking skills.

So you see, even those units that are not typically exciting can be fun, and learning can occur on a more advanced level than just intake. But you probably purchased this book for a different reason. More than likely, you wanted to learn about those other theatre games, right? The ones often associated with improvisation? Well, you still came to the right place. Within the covers of this guide to fun are dozens of the best-loved games, the most useful activities, and the exercises most often employed to tackle various obstacles. Each and every one is designed to make learning more exciting and to make taking the stage less intimidating. So put on your seatbelts, because this is going to be an adventure that will completely alter the geography of your lesson plans.

Chapter 1

Before You Begin

Spotlight on

Mark Lunsford
Franklin Senior High School
Franklin, Louisiana

When asked what he likes most about gaming, Mark Lunsford will tell you that it is about allowing students to feel ready. "Games are fun, a non-threatening way to prepare students for the stage. They teach skills in an enjoyable way that the actors will remember. Later, when the teacher wants the students to recall a particular feeling, he can say, 'Remember when we explored the space to find the lost ring, and I told you that you had to really believe there was a ring in order to perform believably? Well, that is the motivation ...'"

We have all had students who were uncomfortable performing. They are called reluctant learners, and nothing feels better than helping them become self-believers, eager learners, and confident performers. Mr. Lunsford of Franklin Senior High School understands this better than most. Not only does he use games and fun activities to get actors ready for the stage, he uses them to create ensemble, focus, energy, and characterization, just to name a few.

"Sometimes games can be misinterpreted as simply play," he defends, "but that angers me. The truth is, they encourage a high level of thinking." This couldn't be truer! He adds, "I have seen activities help very shy, unmotivated students really shine. It's empowering!" He remembers a freshman, so shy that he found making eye contact painfully difficult and rarely spoke. He must have found theatre comforting, because he stuck with it. After an introductory class, he continued with advanced classes, got parts in shows, and eventually landed a theatre scholarship to Kent State University.

A teacher's triumph may be getting a reluctant learner to act, but confident actors have victories of a different kind. Mr. Lunsford recalls a talented, confident boy. His character was dying of AIDS, but the actor had not quite expressed the needed emotion. "He was to recollect how he lay in a hospital with no visitors, so we used an imaging activity where I took him on this journey in his mind. We walked through 'Admitting,' down a dark hall, past drawn blinds and monitors beeping in the dark. He found the needed emotion and was excellent in the part."

Franklin High School has a very unique yearly program in which actors teach elementary students about children's safety. "The actors use improv to start the scene, then draft outlines for scripts, like in commedia [dell'arte] — just rough outlines, and then we perform for the children. It's a big hit!" Fun, learning, and safety, all in the same activity — clearly a higher level of thinking!

Topics for Discussion

- How have you seen improvisation performed? What types of improvisation were performed? Did you enjoy yourself?
- How is improvisation different from acting in a play?
- What skills might an improvisation actor need more than an actor of plays?
- If your teacher gave you a coconut, a wrench, and a tube of lipstick, how might you create a scene around those items?

Getting Started

You are having a party, but when you pour the can of mixed nuts into the beautifully carved leaded crystal bowl, the last thing to come from the can is a pile of crumbs, salt, and a few stray shell pieces. This unattractive and undesirable mess sits proudly atop your heap of six-dollars-for-a-half-pound snack, threatening to ruin the presentation. But quickly you get rid of the debris, and soon your mixed nuts are ready for the fun.

I hate to tell you this, but there are some crumbs in this book, too. Your students will see them as debris, and they will try to "blow them off." However, as an educator, you know that these tidbits are morsels, not trash, and before your students can truly become improvisational actors, they must learn to appreciate the spice of their art. But, I'll be quick, because we don't want to spoil the party — I mean the fun!

Primarily, students interested in acting games like improvisation and some of the other exercises will need to understand the basic expectations and terminology of the stage. Actors are entertainers, and as such, they need to be heard and seen, and they need to understand fully how to use their craft to relay the intended message of the task at hand.

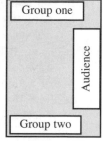

(Diagram 1A)

Why don't we make sure they learn these words by playing a game? First, review the following terminology with your students. Depending on their level of theatre expertise, they will probably know a great deal of the information. Now, break your class into two teams. Line them up on opposite sides of your classroom (as in the game "Red Rover") while you take a seat in the "audience" (see diagram 1A). If the sides are uneven, let the side with the fewest players go first. They will call one player to the middle, and you will ask that player a question, such as "What is a cue?" If he gets it correct, he returns to his team; if he gets it wrong, he goes to the other team. The team with all the players in the end wins. Note: With this game all students win because they all eventually end up on the winning team!

Terminology

Action – all of the movements that take place in a scene

Actor – the real person on stage

Character – the imaginary individual the actor is portraying

Cheat out – to position one's body so that the audience can see

Nick and Cody demonstrate cheating out.

Climax – the point of greatest intensity in the plot

Cue – a signal that tells the actors or a crewmember to do something

Dialog – lines spoken by characters in a play or scene

7

Dramatic structure – a successful scene will follow a structure with a well-defined beginning (the exposition), an obstacle, a climax, and a clear ending

Duet – a scene for two people

En media res – Latin for "in the middle of things," this is a popular way to both insert introductions (after a short "teaser") and begin improvisations (in the middle of conflict)

Exercise – an activity designed to aid the actor in artistic growth

Facial expression – a nonverbal message of the face, eyes, eyebrows, mouth, lips, chin, and so on

Freeze element – a theatrical device in which actors freeze or stand completely still in character until cued to continue their acting normally

Game – an activity intended to aid the actor in achieving artistic advancement but that also includes an element of competition or a fun challenge

Gesture – generally an upper-body movement other than facial expressions that helps the actor to express himself nonverbally

Impromptu – in performance, this means to create or perform "off the top of your head," without taking time to think, or with a very minimal amount of planning time

Improvisation – a scene in which actors make up the dialog and often the story as they go; generally does not involve rehearsals or a script

Mime – an art form in which actors silently express themselves in an exaggerated way, usually while mingling directly with their "audience," the mime artist is usually distinguished with white face makeup and black and white clothing

Mono-improv – an improvised scene with only one actor

Monolog – a scene with one actor (generally rehearsed)

Movement – encompasses everything associated with the actors' bodies, including posture, facial expressions, and all changes in positions and locations

Narrator – a character or person who talks directly to the audience, informing them about events in the play that the actors will not portray; the narrator may also give commentary on a scene, acting almost as a moderator or referee

Pantomime – a scene in which the actor portrays his message using only nonverbal means of communicating; no dialog is used

Posture – the way an actor's body is positioned; this is another form of nonverbal communication

Project – (prō ject) to speak at a volume that will allow all members of the audience to hear

Props – the physical elements of a scene, including things actors carry, pick up, use, or any item used to dress the set

Scene – a part of a larger performance piece that has its own dramatic structure including a beginning, obstacle, climax, and an end

Setting – the geographical location and elements of a scene

Sharing – working with another actor to ensure the successful outcome of a scene rather than working against him or her

Spontaneous – an unplanned action or reaction that appears to happen naturally and without effort

Stage positions – most stages are made up of nine areas (see diagram below); note that directions refer to the actors' left and right when they are on stage facing the audience

U=Up
C=Center
D=Down
R=Right
L=Left

UR	UC	UL
RC	C	LC
DR	DC	DL

the audience

Strategy – a plan for achieving success; in improvisation, actors get only a few moments (if any) to determine quickly how they will make the scene a success, and in many cases, this is worked out as the scene progresses

Teaser – the small part of a scene performed before the introduction when the introduction is not spoken first; the teaser should clearly connect to the main body of the scene, but it does not have to be chronologically ordered

Upstaging – 1. positioning one's self in a way that blocks the audience's view; 2. also referred to as scene stealing, an actor who upstages another is preventing others on stage from getting the attention they need for the scene to be successful

Bianca (in back) should have the audience's focus, but Melissa is upstaging her.

9

Warm-ups – activities used to prepare actors for an upcoming task, usually a performance or a unit requiring a higher level of attention and preparedness; they can vary in form and may include games, improvisation, pantomime, and exercises

The Foundation of Improvisation

Improvisation or *improv* is a type of acting done without a script or rehearsal. An actor or group of actors is given a situation and sometimes characters, and they act out a scene spontaneously, making up the dialog and action as they work their way to a solid conclusion. Part of what makes improvisation enjoyable to the audience is that they know and appreciate that the performance they are watching is being created especially for them. The actors never tire of this spontaneous form of acting, because even if the same basic plot is used over and over, the dialog is always fresh and unique.

There are several different types of improvisational games and activities actors can try to improve their skills and just to have fun, and the number of scenes and types of characters are infinite. However, before your students start improvising, they'll need to know some of the basic ideas that make spontaneous scenes successful. Begin by sharing the following guidelines with them. Afterward, you may want to use the *Understanding Improvisation* worksheet provided later in this chapter to test their understanding.

1. Define your character. Listen to the instructions and do a quick character analysis before taking the stage: How do I walk and talk? How old am I? Do I have any odd habits? How can I use character to make the scene more interesting? Very few actors can just "be themselves" over and over on stage and still demand the audience's attention. Ordinary people just aren't that interesting. The more unique you can make your character, the more likely it is your audience will stay tuned.

Many actors will eventually create a small repetoire of characters that they use over and over again. This is especially true of comedians on weekly TV shows. They find that by bringing the same characters back week after week, they create a continuity that their fans will grow to expect. Likewise, student actors have found that this enables them to fine-tune characterizations, adding depth and dimension to them each time they portray them.

10

2. Be a good listener. Pay attention to the other actors on stage, because their lines are your cue lines, and if the scene lacks good teamwork, it will not be a success. Perhaps the most common mistake young actors make in improv is thinking that they have to talk the whole time or their scene will go nowhere. The opposite is actually true. If you fail to listen, the scene will become so confusing to the audience that they will become restless. Besides, no one wants to hear actors talk over one another, so take turns.

3. Establish where you are: at the mall, the zoo, the beach, or any other place that would enhance the scene. If there is not time to decide on the location before beginning, work it into the skit as close to the beginning as possible. Then the imaginary location can become a part of the scene, giving you more to build on. Trying to make a pizza becomes much more interesting when set in a library instead of in a conventional kitchen.

Melissa and Cody establish that they are at a beach.

4. Know the conflict. Almost all scenes (improvisational or scripted) revolve around a conflict or some sort of obstacle, and if improvisational actors are not clear on what it is, their scene will be confusing to the audience. It is almost always best to try to resolve the conflict as quickly as possible. One rule of thumb is to try three times, the third being successful. Resolving the situation on the first attempt will make the scene uninteresting and too short. Having a second attempt is more interesting but a bit too symmetrical. Resolving it after round three will allow the audience to become interested and engrossed but, with a successful ending, not bored.

Remember that conflict does not mean a fight or even an argument. Most theatre teachers will agree that a very annoying habit of beginning improv actors is to try to turn every improvisation into a hoaky, dramatic morning talk show featuring lines like, "You stole my boyfriend!" This is usually followed by a series of "accusations" and some pushing, and the end result is a boring scene that goes nowhere. A conflict can be something as simple as a fly buzzing around your face while trying to pose for family pictures or something as abstract as two ninjas trying to sneak into a wind chime factory to save a loud-mouthed princess.

5. Pay attention to the instructions of the game or the scene. One of the hardest things to do is play improv games. These are scenes in which you must create a storyline complete with interesting characters and solid dramatic structure *and* complete the requirements of the challenge, too. For example, in *Sit, Stand, and Bend,* the three actors must pay close attention to whether their co-actors are sitting, standing, or bending so that they can fulfill their own objective, *plus* they have to get to the end of the scene. It is easy in games like these either to forget the structure of the scene or to fail to meet the requirements of the game. However, what makes this game so much fun for both the audience and the actors is when a team does both and makes it look easy.

6. Clarify relationships early in the scene if they are not established by the teacher or director. This will help to clear the path for the conclusion. In two-person scenes, what is your relationship to the other character? Are you complete strangers? Are you close? Do you like this person, dislike him, or perhaps envy him? The more your audience is able to decipher, the more they will enjoy the scene.

Including plenty of action will make improvisation more interesting.

7. Include plenty of action in your scenes. Because the audience expects little scenery or props, the actor has it within his power to "pretend" to possess anything he wishes! Good actors can use pantomime to make the audience believe they see a light saber or giant clown shoes. Remember the earlier situation where the person was making pizza in the library? Perhaps he is making the world's largest pizza! Because it is so huge, the actors must stand on opposite sides of it, yell across the room to one another, and walk around it. Perhaps one could accidentally fall in it or drop his tissue (and worse yet — not be able to find it!). Can you imagine the poor guy who has to toss that crust?

8. Keep the scene in the positive rather than the negative. Avoid using responses such as "no." They bring the scene to a sudden halt, whereas responses in the positive — "yes" — keep the scene moving toward the goal and tend to be funnier. Work with your partners instead of against them. If they want something in the scene, no matter how absurd, give it to them. Again, in the scene in which two guys are building the world's largest pizza, one might ask, "Hey, did you remember to bring the pepperoni?" The other could answer in the negative, but then what happens? Nothing. However, if he answers in the positive, the possibilities become endless. "Did I bring the pepperoni? I had to rent a truck just to get it here. The crane's hoisting it up now. Here it comes." And from there, he can guide it in with pantomimed flags or lights, like he's directing traffic at the airport.

With younger players, you will encounter two other forms of negatives: running away and screaming. Sometimes when young actors don't know what to do in a scene, they turn it into a chase. While this may work for about three steps, they will soon discover that there is no place to go but in circles. Metaphorically speaking, that is what will happen to the plot of their scene, too. It will become extremely boring. If this happens, simply stop them and use it as a time to redirect. Remember, this is a learning activity. Never shy away from being the teacher in a scene. Improvisation can be taught, but bad habits — once formed — are hard to break.

9. *Avoid asking questions like "Why?" and "What is that?"* This places the responsibility of the scene on the other actors. They become responsible for continuing the flow of the scene. For example, if you are playing the *Question Game*, even though it is a competitive game, asking why becomes a cop-out. Always try to give your responses some sort of meaningful "body." Instead of asking why, say, "You mean to tell me you want me to stick my head in that lion's mouth? Are you crazy?" As you can see, in an improvisation, the latter response would give more meaning to the scene.

10. *Don't randomly insert nonsensical lines,* for the same reason as above. Oftentimes when students are doing improvisation, they come to a place where they can think of nothing to say. Rather than having silence on stage (which, to young actors, feels very vulnerable), they say something that has nothing to do with the scene. Like a "no" response, this stops the game dead in its tracks. The other player or players will have no logical response. Instead, remember it is not a race. Pause, take a deep breath, and close your eyes if you need to. Allow the others to take the lead if possible. If not, simplify. Do not strive for the funniest

response; simply follow logic. This strategy will allow you to get to a new jumping-off place.

11. Start your scene with a solid conclusion in mind. Coming up with an ending when you are trying to remember if you have to sit or bend and while listening to what the other actors are saying so that you can respond is hard. However, starting your scene knowing the conclusion and working your way toward it is much easier. Sometimes actors get stumped and cannot think of a conclusion for a scene, so it drags on and on. In these cases, a number of troupes will buzz them out or just start clapping (not an admirable way to force a scene to an end, but this is fairly common). You do not want to be buzzed out every time, so practice ending your own scenes. In improvisations where you cannot discuss the ending in advance, try to sense which actors have endings in mind and allow them to lead the way. Never try to take control of a scene if you do not have a solid conclusion. You may be guiding the team away from someone who has a well-planned ending in mind.

Understanding Improvisation Key

1. script, rehearsal
2. dialog, action, ending
3. How do I walk and talk? How old am I? Do I have any odd habits? How can I use character to make the scene more interesting?
4. listeners
5. location
6. conflict
7. objective
8. clear the path for the conclusion
9. action
10. positive, negative
11. Running, screaming
12. Why?, What is that?
13. Pause, take a deep breath, and close your eyes if you need to. Allow the others to take the lead if possible. If not, simplify. Do not strive for the funniest response; simply follow logic. That will allow you to get to a new jumping-off place.
14. solid conclusion

Understanding Improvisation

Do you understand improvisation or improv? Check your understanding by writing the questions and answers on your own paper.

1. Improvisation or improv is a type of impromptu acting done without a _____ or
   _____.

2. The actors are given a scene to act spontaneously, making up the _____ and _____ as they work their way to a solid _____.

3. It is important to quickly define one's character when doing improvisation. What are some things you might decide about characterization before taking the stage?

   _____

   _____

   _____

4. Improvisational actors must be good _____. What others say on stage is important to each actor because it may prompt him or her to say something useful to the outcome of the scene.

5. If there is not time to work it out before taking the stage, establish the _____ of the scene as close to the beginning as possible, then the "surroundings" can be worked into the scene.

6. Know the _____. Almost all scenes involve some struggle, and if you and your partners are not clear on exactly what it is, your scene will be confusing.

7. Pay attention. Whether playing a game or improvising a scene, remember the director's instructions: If there is an _____, keep it in sight.

8. Establish relationships. If relationships are not established by the teacher or director, clarify them early in the scene. This will help to _____.

9. Include plenty of _____. Because the audience expects little scenery or props, the actor has it within his power to "pretend" to possess anything he wishes! Good actors can use pantomime to make the audience believe they see anything.

10. Try to keep the scene in the _____ rather than the _____. Work with your partners instead of against them.

11. _____ away from your improvisation partner on stage is another form of negative, as is _____. Instead, try to find something more meaningful to contribute to the scene.

12. Asking questions like _____ and _____ is another form of negative. It places all the responsibility on your scene partner. Instead, try to respond in a way that will make the scene more interesting.

13. What should you do rather than say something that does not make sense?

   _____

   _____

14. Every improvisation must have a _____ that wraps up the events in the scene.

making Use of What You Know

Knowing terminology is a smart start, but it is not enough. Remember, actors are entertainers, and they have certain things they must do for their performances to be successful. Because this is a book about games and activities, I will not go into great depth on these things. If you are progressing in a logical order, you have already taught these basic skills as a unit prior to attempting improvisation. If not, you may want to back track and cover them before continuing.

Remind actors that there are a few primary goals entertainers and performance artists must remember. The first is that they must be seen. This means that they must assume a position on stage that allows the audience to see their faces and bodies. Imagine the face of a clock placed at Center Stage with 12:00 Up Center and 6:00 Down Center. Obviously, the strongest position for an actor to face regardless of where he stands on the stage would be toward 6:00, because this is "dead center" or full front. Anywhere between 4:30 and 7:30 follow in

Full front

Quarter left

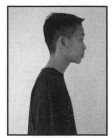

Left profile

Three-quarter left

Full back

strength; they are slightly angled, but still visible to the audience. These positions are referred to as quarter positions. While it is possible that an actor can assume one of the remaining areas and be heard (especially when miked), most directors and actors avoid profile (3:00 and 9:00), three-quarters (1:30 and 10:30), or full back (12:00) because actors cannot be seen. Some exceptions may exist, but they are few, especially in educational theatre.

Besides stage positions and the direction an actor faces, another important part of being seen is stage placement. Down Center is the strongest place for an actor to stand in most cases. Down Right and Left are also strong. However, when a stage has levels, the rules change. Lighting, scenery, and costuming can also change the importance of different placements.

Tell your students that the stage is a lot like the arrangement of a family picture. Normally we put the leaders of the family in the middle and position the children and grandchildren around them. Our eyes are trained to seek out those in the center first, thus the phrase "center of attention." However, our eyes can be tricked to look elsewhere when the photographer uses creativity. If he has everyone in the picture look at the baby in Grandma's arms, then when we look at the picture, we will first look at the baby, also. Likewise, if little McKenzie is wearing red and the rest of the family is in white, we will notice McKenzie right away before scanning the others in the picture. Lastly, if Caden is holding a birthday candle and the family photo is dimly lit, our eyes will be drawn to the candle, and then the child holding it.

However, if no clever devices are used, Down Center is strongest, and Up Right and Left are weakest. Why is this important? Should all the actors struggle to take center? No. They must learn to share the stage. Actors must evaluate who — or in some cases what — is "the center of attention" in a scene. Then they must learn to dress the stage around him, her, or it just like a photographer poses the family so that the audience's focus is on "the center of attention." There is no model for acquiring this skill. It is an art that must be learned. A great way to learn this art is by using the games *Headlines* or *Human Statues*.

Here are some other helpful hints to assist you in staging scenes so that all actors achieve the best visibility:

- Keep hair out of face and wear hats and other costumes so that they do not block your facial expressions
- Follow through with gestures and facial expressions

- Use good eye contact; keep it in the scene when necessary and directed at the audience when required
- Learn when and when not to move; the audience's eyes are drawn to movement
- Explore a wide range of movement, especially in games like *Zap* or *Sit, Stand, and Bend*

Besides being seen, actors must be heard. This means they must articulate clearly and speak strongly and confidently. They must say their lines as though they mean them, and they must learn to manipulate their voices so that they can use believable dialects, interesting voices, and avoid being monotone. Try the vocal exercises in chapter 4 with your classes. They are both fun and effective. Also pass on the following tips:

- Listen to the other actors; if you cannot hear them talk because you are speaking over them, then the audience will become confused
- Speak to the very last row; if they can hear you, so can the rest of the audience

One of the hardest things for young actors to master is effectively conveying the message. This means they must understand the script, or in the case of improvisation, the goal of the scene or game. They need to analyze how each character relates to the others; how the particular time period or locale might affect the movement, the voice, the attitudes, or the delivery; and they need to understand fully the symbolism and the activity's intent. This is easier in improvisation than with a script, because the students are both the creators and the actors. However, do not allow them to become settled with shallow characters, a questionable stage geography (a table that changes places), or a plot that has no clear ending. Encourage them to:

- Give each scene a clear beginning, an obstacle or conflict, rising action, a climax, and a clear ending
- Develop interesting characters and a creative plot
- Follow the rules of the game or activity

Lastly, even a serious game or improvisation must appear to be fun (at least for the actors). When the actors are really involved and having a fun experience, the audience will also be enjoying the show. Keys to achieving this are energy, energy, and more energy:

18

- Top lines, don't think too long, and go with your instincts
- Stay focused on the moment
- Keep it simple
- Do not allow the scene to drag, but don't chop it off without completing the activity
- Gauge your audience; if they become restless, try a new strategy, but always keep the ending in mind

Redirecting

When your students are engaged in a game or scene, remember to stay in control. They are still young, still learning, and there will come many times when they will say or do something that they should not. They may use inappropriate comments or gestures, they may use harmful stereotypes, or they may simply make poor improvisation choices such as those mentioned above. It could be that they stray so far from the goals and objectives of the activity that they need to be put back on the right track.

If this happens, call "cut." I use this word, despite it being somewhat cliché, because I have found that the kids hear it above the noise of a crowded classroom. Whoever originally introduced it into the directors' vernacular must have discovered the same thing. When the kids cannot hear stop, freeze, or quiet, they will still hear cut. Amazingly, they will stop, get quiet, and not move. They know this means business.

After you have their attention, say, "Okay, what is not working here?" Allow them to respond. Then say, "What might they [the performers] have done to have made the scene more interesting [or more successful, etc.]?" Again, let them respond. Chances are there are kids in the audience who were, in their amazingly absorbant brains, trying to fix the scene before you called "cut." Remind them not to be in a hurry, to use listening skills, and to keep the goal in mind. If they are breaking a rule, be sure to correct them. If they are being insensitive, redirect them. If they are using bad improvisation, help them to make a better choice. Then call "action," and let the scene continue. Afterward, discuss any successes they may have had because of the redirection.

Evaluating Games, Improvs, and Exercises

Remembering to incorporate all of the above things can seem overwhelming, but after a few successes, each of these strategies and skills will become second nature. One of the best ways to ensure that your class understands, however, is to train them to be good evaluators. Evaluate improvisations and games? Sure. Although many teachers use them only as icebreakers and to fill nonlecturing time in class, they are recognized as useful and effective acting tools. During the few minutes your students are on the stage for an activity, they will cover most of the fundamentals of acting, and they will also be exploring writing and directing. After all, they are "writing" the script as they go, and they are making all of the creative choices you do when you direct a show from a script.

The *Game and Improvisation Evaluation* later in this chapter is just one kind of improvisation evaluation. It breaks the performance into various acting and gaming goals and allows the teacher to mathematically make his or her judgment about the success of the scene. Even if you choose not to give a grade for the scene, it will be helpful for students to know their strengths and to understand where they need improvement. I recommend never giving a grade below an 80 to students who give a game or other spontaneous activity their all, even if they fall short of the goals. Edmond Guay, theatre teacher at Avondale High School in Auburn Hills, Michigan, points out that, even though all improvisations are not perfect, at least students are on the stage, and that gives you a starting point from which to work with them.

Another thing to consider when evaluating students is to balance your comments in a way that makes them feel that they were more successful than not. I have a policy of saying two positive comments for every criticism I must make. This means that sometimes it becomes necessary not to say everything I want to say in order to preserve students' self-esteem. Perhaps their peers will comment about some of these other items in the peer evaluations. However, everyone needs a fan club, and if young people feel you believe in them, they will try harder. Tell them what to fix, but end with several things they did right. You may find that the other things "fix" themselves!

Examples of Positive Comments Students NEED to Hear (Even If the Scene Did Not Work)
- You had some very good facial expressions.
- That was a very unique and creative idea.
- You had great volume. I heard every word you said.
- There were some very believable moments.
- Your enthusiasm was very apparent.
- There were some nicely detailed pantomimed moments.

- You really seemed to follow the directions.
- You looked like you were having fun!
- You used your space well.
- You did not appear nervous.

Besides the teacher evaluating his or her students, the young people should evaluate one another. This must be done for every performance in writing, and it should be for a grade. It is, I believe, the best learning tool teachers use in their classrooms. A few years ago, a student who had once complained about having to do the peer evaluations, came to me after class to say that she had had an epiphany. Marcella had been working on a scene at home, but she kept feeling that something wasn't right about it. She began skimming through peer evaluations of a recent performance, she found the answer in her own written comments on another student's evaluation. Marcella had noted that, although the scene was good, it was too loud, that there was too much yelling but not enough intensity, so there was never a real climax. She reworked her scene, and instead of yelling, she used a quiet, intense anger. Her peers loved it when she performed two days later, and she was so proud of herself. I felt great knowing that my assignment had helped her to achieve that new understanding.

Peer evaluations can be done on a form (see diagram 1C), but the best and easiest way to do them is on notebook paper. Have students fold their paper down the middle long-ways (some say "like a hotdog bun"). They will write their names at the very top, all the way against the edge of the paper. This is important, because it will help you to allow them to keep their anonymity, which encourages them to be honest. Later, after you have graded and recorded the evaluation, you will cut off the names. Now, on the second blue line, have them write "Strengths" in the first column and "Needs Improvement" in the second. Then, as each student or group performs, they can record the students' initials in the margin, and they can make comments in the columns. Most teachers grade for completion, but you may also want to make sure that the comments they make are appropriate and constructive. After you have graded the evaluations, cut off the students' names and have them sit in a circle. You can now pass the evaluations around and they can read what their peers had to say. This is a great time for discussing performances. You may even want to take this a step further and have them write their peers' comments in their acting journals so that they can refer back to them for making plans for improvement.

21

Name _____ Period _____ Date _____

Peer Performance Evaluation

Give specific information about each performance. You will be graded on completion as well as your ability to phrase comments constructively. Be thorough. **Include a critique of your own performance.**

Performer	This performer was great at ...	But could use a little more work on ...
1. CL	Your intro. was perfect! Great job	Had a hard time hearing you at the end.
2. MT	Nice blocking; good use of stage	Work on memorization.
3. BL	Wow! Super projection/voice	Make intro flow, don't "think" about it
4. NZ	Nice accent, very believable	Articulate through the accent
5. CS	absent	absent
6. LO	Nice articulation, breathing	Pick a piece that isn't so "you"
7.		
8.		

Diagram 1C — The above Peer Evaluation Form and other useful tools may be found in Introduction to Theatre Arts, A 36-Week Action Handbook, by Suzi Zimmerman, Meriwether Publishing Ltd.

This can be a tough time for young actors, because acting is an art and no one likes to be told they are not good. Reinforce throughout the process that all comments must be constructive and viable. In other words, do not allow them to say things like, "That stunk." Make them specifically determine what they did not like and help them to phrase it in a way that will help the actors see where to focus their efforts. At the same time, remind actors that everyone is evaluated every day, and everyone must learn to accept criticism (not necessarily agree with it), and go on with life. Lastly, tell them that good actors use their reviews to make the next performance better, and that every evaluation is a review.

Evaluation Activity

Help students to understand the teacher evaluation form you will use to grade their scenes by allowing them to use it one time. Perhaps you have a videotaped performance of a professional improv troupe or of some of your past sessions. If you are really brave, perform an improvised scene for them and allow them to evaluate you using the form. The best way to comprehend what is expected of one's self is to have the opportunity to apply that knowledge, and the best way to get reluctant actors to the stage is to take that position yourself. After they have used the teacher form, they will then begin using the peer evaluation process described earlier in this chapter.

Name: _____ Date: _____

Name of Activity: _____

Score:

/100

Game and Improvisation Evaluation

For each performance component listed below, circle the number of points you think is appropriate. 1 is the lowest score you can give, and 10 is the highest. Then add the points given and record the total in the box in the right-hand corner. Write any comments in the space provided.

Followed directions
1   2   3   4   5   6   7   8   9   10

Teamwork – Sharing the stage, strategizing
1   2   3   4   5   6   7   8   9   10

Dramatic structure
1   2   3   4   5   6   7   8   9   10

Clear beginning
1   2   3   4   5

Introduced obstacle
1   2   3   4   5

Interesting rising action and climax
1   2   3   4   5

Appropriate ending
1   2   3   4   5

Characterization – Age, attitude, facials, etc.; stayed in character
1   2   3   4   5   6   7   8   9   10

Energetic, entertaining, well paced
1   2   3   4   5   6   7   8   9   10

Voice – Projection, articulation, diction, dialect, quality, etc.
1   2   3   4   5   6   7   8   9   10

Movement – Gestures, posture, props (if allowed), pantomime, etc.
1   2   3   4   5   6   7   8   9   10

Discussion – Actor(s) contributed to a discussion of their performance, accepted criticism, and offered explanations supporting their choices.
1   2   3   4   5   6   7   8   9   10

Comments:

Scene Planning

In this book, some of the activities will include a planning time. This is an independent study time during which students are expected to work toward making each of their scenes successful. If a scene includes this period of preparation, use one of the forms provided or create your own. This is a great time-management tool, allowing students to brainstorm and document their ideas. You may want to consider giving several different grades for this type of activity. The first grade would be for the completed worksheet. Second, students would be graded on their performances, and lastly, they would be graded on their evaluations of their peers. Other options include averaging the three grades to make one "test" or "performance" grade and adding an audience grade based on how well they demonstrated appropriate audience behavior.

• Remember to give a grade for demonstrating appropriate audience skills anytime your students watch a performance.

By providing a worksheet for the preparation, students become much more accountable for the outcome of their scenes. You have heard excuses in the past such as, "You didn't give us enough time," or "We worked really hard, but we couldn't come up with anything." The preparation form will always include a space at the bottom for teacher comments, and this will help you to reply to those excuses in the off-chance a student still tries to use them. You might note, "This group spent ten minutes trying to find paper and pens." After reading that, it would be unreasonable for anyone to think they still had justification for complaining.

Furthermore, when a student is forced to write ideas, their tiny sparks of creativity are allowed to shine brighter. After making several notes, odd combinations begin to form. Once when writing a play with my students, we brainstormed topics for the main idea. Our list included "superheroes," and on another page, someone had scribbled "support group." When we went back over our ideas, one of the students who was writing her favorites accidentally wrote "superhero support group" on the same line. We laughed about her mistake, considered the absurdity of the topic, and before long, we were all stuck on that as the central idea for our play. Had we not written our "brainstorming" ideas, the accidental combination of topics would never have become a three-act play.

These planning sheets also make wonderful reference tools for the future. Oftentimes, students will look at past sheets to get ideas for their latest scenes. They also share worksheets with other students. You can even create a "Wall of Fame" on a bulletin board of "famous" scenes, unused (but definitely viable) topics, and pictures of your students in action. You never know when an old notion will spark new creativity in a student who thought she would never come up with an idea for a scene.

For games that do not require a planning time, consider modifying them slightly for beginners. For example, if you are playing *Party Crashers*, let your students write down some ideas first, even though it is not a requirement. This will give them confidence to take the stage knowing that they will not go blank. As always, discuss each one afterward, and encourage students to talk about what they thought did and didn't work about their own performances. In the early stages of improv, it is better to do self-evaluations aloud, and only use written peer evaluations. You may even decide not to let students see what their peers had to say about them if they are having confidence issues (unless, of course, it will boost their confidence). With students in the intermediate stages of acting, you can make taking preparation and planning notes optional, and allow oral peer evaluations afterward. As your students become more advanced, tell them that they do not need to make planning notes but that they can record the activities and results in their journals on their own time. This will force them to become more spontaneous actors and thinkers, but it will also give them a short leash for returning to the safety and security of their written work.

Sample form

Generic Activity Planning Guide

Name of Activity:_____ Date: _____
Names of Students in Group: _____

Directions: _____
_____
_____
_____

Goal/Objective: _____
_____

You will have _____ minutes to plan this activity. It is due _____.

Teacher Notes, Questions, Comments:

Plot Ideas – What will your scene be about? Circle your final choice.

1.   5.
2.   6.
3.   7.
4.   8.

Setting Ideas – Where will your scene take place? Circle your final choice.

1.   5.
2.   6.
3.   7.
4.   8.

Obstacles – To add interest, something stands between you and your goals. What might that be?
Circle your final choice.

1.   5.
2.   6.
3.   7.
4.   8.

Sample form

Scene Summary
Our scene starts when ...

Then ...

And it gets really interesting when ...

Finally ...

Characterizations

Actors in Group	Voice (if not pantomimed)	Posture	Habits	Attitude
1.				
2.				
3.				
4.				
5.				

After the performance, each member should respond in the space provided
Was your scene a success? Explain.
1.
2.
3.
4.
5.

If you could change one thing, what would it be and why?
1.
2.
3.
4.
5.

If your peers orally critiqued your performance, what were some of the things they liked? (One person may respond.)

What were some of the things they would have like to have seen changed? (One person may respond.)

27

Discussion Strategies

My favorite way to hold classroom discussions is like King Arthur held his round table, in a circle. This way every student faces every other student, and the teacher is on the same level. Those who would rather not pay attention have no other choice. Also, everyone is in full view, so passing notes, doing homework, or dozing are not options.

Many teachers use a ball or bean bag to denote who may talk. This is a nice way to ensure that each student has his turn and is not interrupted. You may also work your way around the circle, use a timer, or tell students they can talk using one breath, and when they run out of breath, they have to pass to the student next to them. With smaller groups, you will probably be able to relax and just let them talk. However, with larger groups, tricks like these will keep the comments short and sweet and give everyone a chance to participate in the discussion.

If you are holding one discussion after all performances are finished, then the above round-table method will work. However, if you are critiquing each performance immediately afterward, you will need a different strategy. Allow the performer to ask the questions (below). You can help encourage certain types of comments by asking questions, such as "Nick, what did you think of Michael's articulation?" This is especially useful when you know a student has made great improvement or that she is a good model for other students' articulation difficulties. Set a minimum number of responses, and try to balance each negative comment with at least two positives. If it appears that the audience is too negative, find a way to redirect them, "Wow! What about that topic, Courtnie?" Or go to the next student: "We are running out of time, so record any additional comments in your journals." You do not want to discourage the performer being evaluated.

Here are some discussion starters for evaluating scenes and spontaneous acting:

- What worked in this scene?
- Was there anything that didn't work?
- Were you able to see a clear plan?
- Did the actors follow the rules of the assignment?
- Did the scene flow well (did it have a beginning, an obstacle, rising action, climax, and clear ending)?
- Was the scene a success?
- How can the actors improve for next time?

And for group scenes:

- Did the company of actors have good teamwork?
- Any of the above questions

Spontaneous Acting Journals

Many theatre teachers require students to keep an acting journal, so it will be simple to add a section for spontaneous acting. This is a good place for students to record how to play each game, whether they liked it or not, and what they learned. During oral peer evaluations and later when they get to look at the written peer evaluations, they can record what their co-actors had to say about their performance.

There are over 100 activities in this book, including the modified versions, and thousands more on the Internet and in other books. You probably have many that are not included here, and students will learn dozens more over the years. Keeping a journal, while a smart artistic move, is also imperative for keeping up with the multitudes of activities that exist. It will also offer another opportunity for you, the teacher, to check students' understanding, evaluate their likes and dislikes, and to record a grade.

Lesson Plans and Semester Syllabus

When introducing games to the classroom, many teachers become stumped with how often to play them, how long, and how to justify a "game" on the lesson plan. The following three days of lesson plans and a brief suggested semester syllabus will help to clear up any confusion you may have.

Also, use the *Target Areas Index*, to find useful activities to support the daily objectives of some of your regular lessons. For example, when teaching about articulation, consider using the vocal exercises in chapter 4, and when teaching about teamwork, play *The Bridge* later in the same chapter. It is probably wise to introduce spontaneous acting activities as a unit, but then include the various fun activities as parts of other units to boost learning.

Sample Lesson Plans

Date: 9/7	Bell Work: In life, we know that sharing is important. Why is it important for actors to "share" the space on stage? Discussion.
Objective:	Today students will review the various areas of the stage, abbreviations for these areas, and how to write basic script scoring for these in their scripts.
Lesson:	Using a transparency of stage areas, students will learn about the stage.
Activity:	Take students on tour of a stage including demonstrating how each area is lit. Allow students to experience the way the various areas feel as far as "importance" goes (for tomorrow's lesson).
Assessment:	*Stage Maps:* Students will draw a card containing various stage directions; they must show me that they understand by following the directions on their card. Quiz students with diagram, labeling.
Homework:	Look at your family pictures. How are people arranged? Who is in the middle? Where is everyone looking? Is this the most interesting arrangement? What catches your attention? Write one paragraph.
Date: 9/8	Bell Work: Yesterday you learned about stage areas. In your opinion, in which areas can the actor be most easily seen by the audience and why? Which areas make it hard to see the actors and why? Discussion.
Objective:	Today students will discover the importance of each stage area and how to dress the stage. They will explore color, lighting, movement, position, eye contact, and levels and how each affects the direction in which the audience's eye is drawn.
Lesson:	Discussion: Regarding family pictures, how were the people arranged? Who was in the middle? Where was everyone looking? Was this the most interesting arrangement? What caught your attention?
Activity:	*Headlines:* Students will create human pictures to accompany newspaper headlines in an attempt to force focus and demonstrate a message.
Assessment:	I will take pictures and we will discuss and evaluate the "human pictures" as a class.
Homework:	None tonight.
Date: 9/9	Bell Work: Talk about yesterday's *Headlines* activity. Which two or three human photographs stood out in your mind? Why? Now discuss how those same qualities translate to a play production. How can actors and directors use the qualities you mentioned (not the stage pictures) to improve productions?
Objective:	Today students will learn the basics of blocking, including crossing, countercrossing, using the space, and scoring these movements in a script.
Lesson:	Brief overview of objective followed by discussion, Q & A, and reteaching.
Activity:	*Buzzer Game:* Students will write their co-actors' blocking for a few of the scenes as the class plays the game and we will discuss. As soon as it is apparent that all understand the activity, we will continue the game for fun. May also play *Zap*, another great movement game.
Assessment:	During discussion, it will be apparent if students are grasping the basics of blocking. However, to be sure, I will have them complete an *Activity Evaluation* and include their scoring of their blocking on the back.
Homework:	Watch how your teachers lecture "to the audience." What skills do they use that are also taught in this class? Do you think other professionals use some of these same skills? Explain in one paragraph, due tomorrow. Current Theatre Event also due tomorrow. Don't forget to outline.

Suggested Semester Syllabus

Week 1: Use getting-to-know-you games while establishing your class structure, rules, and expectations. Have fun, but also set a serious tone for learning, and make sure students understand that in order to play the fun games they must commit to completing the not-so-fun work first. These games will help to break the ice:

10. *Near and Dear*
44. *Garden of Statues*
46. *You Started It!*

Weeks 2–6: Continue playing a few getting-to-know-you games when time allows, but focus on the basics of theatre, too. Introduce some simple activities as you feel they are ready. This will get them used to the stage or the performance area. If they are eager to perform, assign a few of the silent scenes. These have little or no speaking, so they are wonderfully easy for beginning actors. Some great activities for this time might include:

1. and 2. *Just Kidding*
3. *The Story of My Life*
40. *Killer*
75. *What Are You Doing?*
78. *Silent Scene*

Weeks 7–9: Students are ready to begin some serious acting. Assign monologs or duets, and then play some of the fabulous games that support scene work. These will help students both to understand their scenes and to develop multidimensional characters. However, at this time, you might also start inserting some of the independently creative games in which students are in charge of the outcome:

4. *Ta-Da!*
7. *Vocal Warm-up*
22. *Frames*
30. *The Three Energies*
65. *Murder Mystery*

Weeks 10–12: Students should really be blossoming as young performers. It's time to tap into the more deeply artistic person inside.

31

These activities will stir their imaginations and make them eager to try new things:

26. *Pioneers*
35. *The Buzzer Game*
64. *Two-ringed Improvisation*
76. *Mystery Catch*

Weeks 13–18: If you have a one-semester course, this is the final passageway. Assign new scenes for your final exams, and get your students ready for their last performances (at least of the semester) by introducing them to the more advanced games and activities:

9. *Taking a Walk*
25. *Concentration Circle*
43. *Forgot My Own Name!*
48. *Scenes for Dealing with Social Issues*

Is It a Game, Improv, or Exercise?

Oftentimes, those outside of theatre do not understand the differences between games, improvisations, and exercises. They are all fun, but they all have distinctly different objectives and definitions.

A theatre *game* is more competitive in nature, and it usually does not revolve around a plot. Some involve acting and some do not, and while they still require a high level of creative thinking, they are not usually conducive to developing deep characters or following a dramatic structure. These will rarely have "winners," but some will. Most often, even though the activity is competitive, the success of actors is subjective and varies depending on the audience. In other words, one audience member may have liked a different actor's performance than the person sitting next to him. At the same time, the teacher may have favored another actor altogether. Remind students that it is unimportant who did "the best," but what is vital is that all students are growing as actors.

There are a huge number of common kids' games like *Red Rover* and *Red Light, Green Light* that acting teachers will use as getting-to-know-you games or for fostering attention, movement, or some other skill. It is imperative that the teacher involve students in discussion about how these games relate to the task at hand. Otherwise, students will think that the teacher is wasting time or bored with acting. It is always vital to engage students in this type of discussion, but even more so when the lines between productivity and sheer fun become harder to define.

An *improvisation* is a form of acting done without a script and with little or no rehearsal. To *improvise* is to invent as the plot progresses. In commedia dell'arte in sixteenth-century Italy, actors improvised their lines while adhering to a basic plot and portraying stock characters. Today, improvisational actors may still use a common storyline, but in most cases, even that is decided at the last minute.

In most improv, actors are given a situation, and in some cases, they may also be given a setting and/or characters. From that, they must create a scene on the spot. In almost every case, improv is combined with some sort of fun challenge, which may be why so many people confuse improvisation with gaming.

> **Here's a bright idea ...**
> For starting actors, it may be better to allow two minutes off stage to discuss their scene before performing. At the same time, if you have students waiting, this can either be lost learning time for them or a chance to play a quick game of one-minute Charades. This will keep them tuned in to the lesson while the next group to perform plans.

Lastly, an *exercise* is an activity intended to improve some area of a production or performance needing additional focus. These, too, can be very fun, which is why people may confuse them with games. They can also involve acting, so people confusie them with improvisation. Exercises may be used to improve memorization, energy, focus, dialect, articulation, breathing control, camaraderie, and movement, just to name a few.

Timing is extremely important when using exercises, many of which are also warm-ups. Most directors use them before rehearsals so that the learning can support that day's objectives. When used often enough, the learning becomes second nature.

Pantomime and mime, two forms of acting that may or may not be improvised, will also be covered in some detail in this book. *Pantomime* is acting out a task without using props; there is generally no restriction on speaking. *Mime*, on the other hand, is an art form in which actors create an entire environment, including props, obstacles, and often a short plot, by using exaggeratedly crisp movements. The mime artist does not speak, portraying his entire message clearly with movement *and* by tapping into the audience's desire to want to believe what they cannot see. Mimes are usually associated with white facial makeup and black and white clothing.

Both mime and pantomime can be used in many of the games, exercises, and improvisations in this book, and there are a number of activities designed specifically for "the silent actor."

The Importance of Gaming and Improvisation

You might ask yourself, "Why do I want to introduce a loud, action-oriented element into my orderly classroom?" There are many reasons, and the first is that no theatre classroom should always be quiet. Second, not every game is loud. If you have ever had the pleasure of visiting a school band hall, you have witnessed firsthand the cacophony of sounds that various instruments in the hands of energetic young artists can create. Likewise, the oofs, splats, cracks, and smacks of an athletic field require no explanation. Drama teachers are not just passing on information; they are motivating, inspiring, and stirring their students. The reward will be when those same students take the stage and begin making noise, moving, jumping, crawling, and becoming.

Another reason to play creativity games with students is that at most schools theatre is an elective. From a list of potential classes, students choose the one they wish to take. If a class has good numbers, more classes will be created for that teacher. If he or she has poor numbers, that teacher will likely end up teaching stray classes in some field unrelated to fine arts. The way to make your class desirable so that students will elect to take it is to make it both fun and educational. Gaming and improvisation are both terrific and proven ways to accomplish this goal.

While there are innumerable reasons for making the drama room fun, most drama teachers agree that the most important reason is this one: Practicing spontaneous acting activities will make your students greater actors, more scholastically prepared, and they will become more savvy professionals. The reason? They learn to think creatively on their toes. Improvisation is a wonderful training tool, arming students for situations in which a person must decide in an instant how to react. Games create a competitive atmosphere that makes everyone strive to do better. Sure, your classroom may be less structured, but it will be productive, and your legacy as a fun and motivational teacher will continue in your students.

For a list of suggested books and websites to help you implement theatre games in the classroom see the resources section in the back of this book.

Spontaneous Acting Projects

Introduce the following projects to your students and have each select one to be completed and presented to the class. Instruct students to be neat and show a great deal of effort. Decide in advance how large each group may be depending on your particular students and the difficulty level of each individual assignment. You may want to vary the difficulty level for students who wish to work alone (thirty-five or fifty lines or pictures for projects three and four) or for larger groups.

Project One: Make an **instructional video** teaching your fellow students how to play a particular improvisational game or activity. The video should be well organized and cleanly pieced together. Several people may participate.

The finished product must include on-screen credits and an on-screen title that includes the name of the activity. These can be done with electronic graphics, on posters, or using some other, more creative method. Also include where you found the game, a list of materials needed to play the game, an explanation of how many can play, and of course instructions and/or rules for playing the game successfully. Lastly, include a successful sample of the activity in which your group plays the game. If your game requires a larger number of people than are in your group, you may include friends or family members. End your video with your group discussing how this particular activity is useful to theatre.

Project Two: Create an **improvisation notebook** that clearly instructs the reader how to play ten improvisation games or activities. The notebook should be neat and well organized. All of the material must be in the student's own words and format. *Do not copy and paste from the Internet!*

The finished product must include a title on the cover. Inside, include a cover page with the title, the project name and number, the names of your group's members, the source for the activity (where you found it), and the date the project is due. After the cover page, you will have ten pages, one for each game. On each of these ten pages, include a title for each game, a list of materials needed to play, an explanation of how many may play, and of course instructions and/or rules for playing the game successfully. End each page by discussing how your group thinks this particular activity is useful to theatre.

Project Three: Create a list of **100 famous lines,** sayings, slogans, mottos, or lyrics for the *Whose Line Is Next?* game. The lines must be neatly typed and triple-spaced on clean paper. Make sure the lines are appropriate for class. Ask classmates, parents, and teachers for their suggestions. (Teachers, you may want to save the time of having to cut these out by having students write them neatly on index cards. At the same time, by having students type them, you can always make multiple copies and keep them filed away for future use.) When possible, cite the source of your lines (who said them).

Project Four: Gather **100 pictures** of people, animals, and items to be used in *The Picture Game.* Cut them out neatly and mount each to a clean piece of typing or construction paper. The pictures must be appropriate for class. (Teachers, you may want to specify that the mounting paper all be the same size for easy filing.)

Chapter 2

Preparing

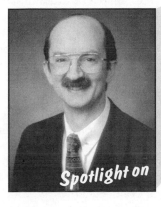

Dr. Len Radin
Drury Drama Team
Drury High School
Spotlight on   North Adams, Massachusetts

In the world of theatre, a teacher with "Dr." in front of his name usually refers to someone who has studied the finer points of theatre and braved the lengthy doctoral studies program. In general, he is devoted to the arts and has superior creativity. This lover of theatre is also extremely intelligent.

Drury High School in North Adams, Massachesetts, boasts a different kind of doctor in its high school theatre department. He is a special educator who knows theatre, has braved many years in college, and is devoted, creative, and very smart. However, instead of wielding a PhD, he is armed to the tooth, so to speak, with a different set of letters. He is Dr. Len Radin, DDS — a dentist.

Doc, as he is affectionately called, knows a lot about theatre. After all, he is the Massachusetts State Thespian Director and has been inducted into the Educational Theatre Association's Hall of Fame. But more than theatre and dentistry, Doc loves his students. He is a volunteer theatre teacher and director, teaching several classes each week at Drury High School in North Adams, Massachusetts, on top of running a busy dental practice.

He tells about one particular student — we will call him Kurt — who entered his program as a freshman struggling to read. Kurt had a tough year, and it just seemed to get worse as time went on. Fate brought Kurt and Doc together outside the classroom when the young man was arrested for breaking into Doc's dental practice and stealing a tank of nitrous oxide (laughing gas). Police were able to follow the trail of blue paint left as the heavy blue tank was dragged along the ground. At the other end of the trail, they found the unconscious teen.

The judge asked Doc what he wanted to happen to the student, and the teacher replied that he wanted to see him stay in school and to get off drugs. This must have been the perfect prescription, because Kurt did just that. He followed the doctor's orders, stayed in school, stayed off drugs, and became deeply involved in the theatre program, going on to star in several shows.

A few years later, Doc took some students to the state Thespian convention. The organizers had asked him to lead the group in a game, and he obliged. He had a game for a large audience, a sort of icebreaker. In this activity, Doc would stand on stage in front of the 700-plus young people and say something like, "I am from the state of Connecticut." Everyone in the audience who was also from that place would reply by standing and shouting, "I am from the state of Connecticut" (refer to the instructions in chapter 4 for more information on the game *I Am*).

On his way to the stage to start the activity, Doc saw his student in the first row. As he passed by, he whispered, "Kurt, you are from the planet Saturn." Without hesitation, Kurt replied with a matter-of-fact "yes."

"What he meant," Doc would later recount, "was 'Who knows where I would be without theatre and teachers who cared. If Doc says I am from Saturn, I can look up and I see rings and I see Titan, Prometheus, Pan, and Phoebe and all the other beautiful moons of Saturn and they move me to tears. It's exciting and safe in this place.'" And as the game progressed and Doc cued him, Kurt stood and proudly announced that he was from the planet Saturn. What he meant — what his theatre teacher and those who have never met Kurt will tell you he was saying is, "I'm glad I'm alive. Thank you, thank you, thank you, teachers."

Today, Kurt continues to stay clean and is very deeply involved in theatre and professional acting. Dr. Len Radin is still mending broken teeth, leading an impressive drama team, and inspiring students to achieve more than they dreamt possible. Smile, Doc! Your legacy lives on.

Topics for Discussion

- Look around your acting space. Do you see things that might be hazardous to fast-moving games? Make note of anything that might cause an actor to hurt himself, and tell how this could be quickly remedied.

- Playing theatre games, performing improvisations, and doing the other activities in this book require a great deal of self-discipline. What are some behaviors that might interfere with the class's learning? What are some ground rules that the group should agree upon before starting? Why is it important to set up rules prior to starting this type of energetic activity?

Getting Started

Safety

Safety is the paramount issue when playing these fun activities. It is the teacher's responsibility to know her classroom, to understand the hazards, and to ensure that everything is done to create a safe climate for the fun and energetic learning ahead. Students also need to pitch in to ensure that everything is done to make their learning environment safe.

Finding enough space to allow all your students to swing their arms at the same time without touching another can be difficult. For some games, they will also need to be able to lie down on the floor with arms outstretched, maintaining enough personal space that they do not interfere with others. If you take your students to the stage to do these activities or if you are lucky enough to have a stage in your classroom, you will probably have all the room you need. Position yourself between the students and the edge of the stage and redirect students who get too close. This is especially important in games in which running or darkness is involved. However, most teachers will do these activities in their classrooms, and while the space is less flexible, it is usually more conducive to the high levels of energy you will witness.

Move all desks to the sides or back, and get rid of cords strung across the floor. When you can provide advanced notice, tell students to wear comfortable clothing and jazz shoes or sneakers. Otherwise, just have them remove their clunky or loose-fitting shoes.

As an added precaution, you may want to tape off a safety zone with colored spiking tape. Tell students to stay inside the taped area and away from desks and walls. You can tell them (in certain activities) that those who step out must sit out for the remainder of the activity. Other things that can be dangerous are purse straps on the floor, things hanging from the ceiling, and sharp edges. It sounds like you are preparing for a battle, but it is really just common sense. A football coach would not send a student to the line-up without pads, nor would a dance teacher allow her students to dance around taped down electrical cords. You are simply creating a safe place for an energetic activity.

Establishing Rules

Besides making the space safe, you must prepare the young people who will be involved. Create rules for acting activities much like those you probably have for your regular class time. Because you are dealing with more mature students, some of the rules are no longer mentioned on a daily basis as they were when your students were in the lower grades. For example, you probably do not find yourself having to say "no pushing" quite as often as a teacher whose students are younger, but in these games, it is an imperative rule. The following are a suggested body of guidelines for spontaneous acting activities:

Rules for High-Energy Activities
- Follow the rules of the activity
- Keep it clean — avoid profanity and "bathroom" humor
- Respect your co-actors, the teacher, and your audience
- Stay in the acting/audience space
- Know your limitations, and respect others' limitations

By having students follow the rules of the activity, they will gain maximum benefits and avoid hurting themselves or others. Because every setting and group of students are different, you may want to note in the margins of the book when a game does not work well with your class or when it pushes the limitations of your performance space. In those cases, you can make adjustments to the game, the room, or simply remember not to use that activity for the remainder of the year.

Monitoring Prep Time

Monitor independent working time closely. Rather than sitting or perching yourself at the edge of the group, walk among them, talk to them, offer suggestions and praise, and if you notice they are off task, redirect them. If they are using worksheets for their planning time, make notes on the worksheet about their progress. When they see you write a comment like, "Looks like your group isn't making the best use of your time," they will know that their time usage will affect their grade. At the same time, positive comments like, "I am seeing some high levels of thinking and creativity from this group," will encourage students to continue the hard work and may inspire them to raise their own bar.

Monitoring Content

Due to some games' frenzied pace, spontaneity, and because older students' hormones are in maximum working order, you will probably encounter sexual matter, cursing, items that are socially insensitive, and many statements that may be deemed politically incorrect. Theatre is one of the greatest art forms because it does allow us to explore and question our beliefs, but at the same time, you are dealing with young people. Have students talk about what they do and do not want to see and hear in their classroom. Make a list of topics that are in the *sensitive zone*, and discuss why some students may be offended. Suggest that using them as the basis of an improvisation might help others to understand differing points of view. In the end, honor students' requests and require the class to avoid compromising subjects. At the middle or high school level, *never let students include inappropriate matter in their improvisations or games.*

All the Bells and Whistles

Now that you have a large, hazard-free space and a solid set of ground rules, you need to have the bells and whistles — literally. Some of the games call for buzzers, and these are fairly easy to make. Check with your local hardware store, your parents' organization, or maybe your school's technology department. If this is too much trouble, substitute a bell or a whistle, or you can even make a buzzer sound with your mouth.

Game Pieces: Stock up on spare board game pieces, spinners, and dice. Sometimes the play money, cards, and game boards are useful, too. As a fun project, have students make large spinners that can be seen from all corners of your classroom, or have them make a pair of giant dice in their costuming class out of fabric and batting.

Prop Box: There are a number of games for which a prepared prop box is needed. For these, you will want to keep a large box of hats, glasses, wigs, and other props and costume pieces that can instantly inspire a character, a setting, or an idea. Some popular items to include are:

- Anything "old-fashioned"
- Boas, large purses, Halloween costume pieces and masks
- Nondescript items that could be used for a number of things, such as broom handles or lamp shades
- Popular props, such as phones, crutches, a cane, or a microphone
- Clown costume pieces
- Anything oversized or exaggerated (for instance, those giant wooden spoon and fork wall hangings)
- Rubber chickens, chattering teeth, and other comedy mainstays
- Toys (plastic lawn mower, giant plastic scissors, doctor's kits, play makeup, and so on)
- Miscellaneous odd objects, such as unusually shaped foam, unidentifiable tools, and items from other cultures or regions

If you do not have a budget for these items, request donations from your fellow teachers or send students on a *Prop Scavenger Hunt* (see chapter 8 for more information on the *Prop Scavenger Hunt*).

Picture and Headline File: Prepare a file box of pictures, headlines, product taglines, and articles for use in a variety of games and as helpful writing prompts. Have students and your fellow teachers donate pictures or outstanding bits of text from magazines, papers, or from the Internet, and mount each to an 8" X 10" piece of paper so that they will all be the same size. You may even color code them according to category. This makes storage and maintenance easier, especially if you have them laminated to preserve them for future use. Pictures can be of people, animals, places, or objects, or they can be headings or advertisements. They can be funny or serious, and as long as they inspire a feeling or an idea, every picture and bit of text will have a use. Articles, headlines, and taglines should inspire a visual image or a strong emotion. Sort the collected items in the following categories: males, females, groups of two or more, animals, objects, headlines, taglines, articles, and miscellaneous.

Art Supplies: You will find that a stock of art supplies will also be handy, but they will be used quickly. Keep a box of scissors, glue, paper, glitter, sequins, pom pons, and other art supplies for projects like the *Character Collage.* At the start of the year, have students donate one thing for the box or allow them to furnish their own items at the time of need. With these supplies and with all of your props, costumes, and set items, come up with a creative way to ensure that you will not lose these things permanently. Students may leave class without their house key because they will forget it, but they will probably not forget their shoe. Requiring them to exchange it for art supplies is one way to guarantee you will get back what is yours. You could also keep a list, but there is no promise that they will return the item if there is no penalty for losing track of it.

Gauging Time

Now that you have prepared the space, collected some great prompts, and given your students parameters within which to work, there are a few other things to consider. Most games do not take much time, and a great deal will depend on how many repetitions you choose to do of each one. For warm-ups and most exercises, you will want to set aside about fifteen minutes or more. These tend to take less time because the entire group usually participates simultaneously. Games also tend to go quickly because most are for large groups and they are fast-paced. Improvisations, pantomimes, and mimes will require more time. Before each activity, you will find an estimate for how long each game will take. Remember, this will vary from group to group.

The best way to gauge how much time is needed is to define clearly what you hope to gain. For example, if you are trying to increase students' energy, then play games until they are energetic — but not until they are worn out. If you are trying to focus the group, to get them to concentrate on the moment, then work until they are comfortably at that point. If you push them past the objective, they will begin daydreaming, and this defeats the purpose.

Certain games and activities offer immeasurable possibilities for students, and if you do not set limits, they could go on for way too long. Set time limits for how long they have to prepare. Remind them how much time they have remaining, and when it gets down to the last few minutes, tell them to wrap up their planning. It is also important to set time limits for their performances. For example, for a silent scene, it would be easy for a student to get ready for school in twenty seconds, while in real life, they spend a half hour. Obviously neither will work, so tell them that you want to see at least two minutes but no more than five. This will force them to put more thought and planning into the activity.

Props

You will also find that it is important to set limits as to what they can use in their scenes. Most agree that a chair or two should suffice in scene work. This should be enough for most games, too. Many theatre teachers have wooden cubes in their classrooms. These make the best set pieces because they can be arranged to be a table and chairs, a filing cabinet, a sofa, or a wall. They are about the size of the little storage crates (like milk crates) popular at college campuses. They are light-weight, sturdy, and they stack, so if you do not have the wooden cubes, you may want to purchase several of the little plastic milk or file crates.

Grouping Students

One necessary activity that always proves to be a chaotic time-waster is breaking students into cooperative learning groups. The most obvious way is to let them make their own groups. This may work once or even twice, but after that, you will always see the same students in similar scenes with similar acting styles. The best way to pair students off or to break them into small groups is to match strengths to weaknesses. For example, if student A has problems with time management and student B is an organized planner, they might make a great pair. However, monitor them closely to ensure that B is not doing all the work; instead, they should be learning from one another. Point out A's strengths and what he can bring to the group. Then make sure he is doing his part.

Another creative way to break your class into groups is to use their birthdays. If you need four groups, then A is the January through March group, B is the April through June group, and so on. It may or may not be important to have each the same size. If so, improvise. Some teachers use the random method of name drawing. Lastly, try grouping students who have never worked together before or who share similar interests but do not sit together. This can be a great way to foster new friendships.

Deciding Performance Order

Besides breaking students into cooperative learning groups, deciding on performance order can also become chaotic and time-consuming. The following suggestion has always worked for me: On the day of performances, pass out the *Game and Improvisation Evaluation*. Instruct students to fill out the top, and then start taking volunteers. I encourage students to volunteer by giving bonus points, five to the first volunteer, four to the second, three to the third, and two to anyone else who volunteers. As each raises his hand, I assign him a number and he writes it on his sheet in the upper right-hand corner, then passes it to me. I keep them in order. If several want to go first, I draw from those randomly and give them all 5 points. When students stop volunteering, I have those who did not get a number pass their sheets in. I always say, "If you do not turn in your evaluation sheet now, you will become a volunteer." When I am sure all the remaining sheets are in, I randomly draw from them and announce the name and number. These students do not get bonus points. Do not forget to include students who are absent. They should be placed at the end, but when they return, you can give them the option of volunteering. At that time, insert them anywhere, but do not reduce anyone's volunteer points.

This works well because students have a choice about when they will perform. If performances span across several class times, then those who were not prepared the first day have no reason to be still unprepared by the time their names are called. If they are still not ready, it was their choice rather than just bad luck.

Audience Etiquette

Your students are almost ready to take the stage, but before they do, is their audience ready? Do they understand how their presence can impact the performance? Read and discuss the following guidelines with your students. Review them regularly, and post them everywhere in and around your performance area. Encourage them to discuss times when an audience may have changed the course of a show. As the "rules" are broken, discuss them again. There are some rules that will not apply to your group, but they will apply in real-life settings, such as going to the movies, so review them all. As theatre arts teachers, raising appreciative and informed audience members should be high on our list of priorities.

- Students will go to the restroom and get drinks prior to the performance
- Students will sit upright in their seats
- If students must write during the performance, they will have all needed materials out before the first performer takes the stage
- Students will remain appropriately quiet during the performance
- Students will laugh and clap appropriately
- Students will reserve constructive criticism for group discussions led by the teacher; outside the discussion group, students should never try to direct fellow actors unless assigned as the leader of a student-directed project

45

True, Unbelievable Stories of Good Audiences Gone Bad

Both actors and the audience may be distracted by a number of things. Papers rattling or a student digging through her backpack can ruin the mood of a scene or throw an actor out of focus. Even a little harmless silent movement can throw a successful scene into a violent downward spiral. The following distractions actually happened to me and my students. Perhaps you can add your own horror stories to the list. Discuss the incidents with your classes. They will probably find them ludicrous and hard to believe, but each is true. Use them as learning opportunities so that you and your students can avoid similar performance disasters.

During any given school assembly, I will generally collect several small flashlights and laser pointers, a number of hand-held video game devices, and several tissues full of gum (the kind that pops loud bubbles, of course) and candy. If the seats are springy or squeaky, there will be a few eager audience "performers" who will entertain their friends by attempting to be louder than the actors.  Then there are those who will prop their feet up on the seat in front of them, those who will attempt to do homework, and the usual sleepers (and snorers). Sometimes managing the misbehavior becomes more of a distraction, so sternly discussing expectations with the students ahead of time and offering a solid adult presence

Bad audience.

is better than trying to deal with students during a performance.

Cell phones and pagers are another big distraction! During our musical a few years ago, a parent left his cell phone on despite our request in the program to "please turn all cell phones and pagers off." Not only did it ring, he answered it and carried on a three-minute conversation without ever leaving his seat.

Good audience.

In live theatre, babies and small children will do better at a sitter's. When my students did Shakespearean scenes as a performance, I performed with them in the role of Katherine in a scene from *The Taming of the Shrew.* My family was late to the performance

46

and came in during my scene. My son, then three, saw me on stage and excitedly began telling everyone that that was his mommy. He ended his "monolog" by yelling, "Hi, Mommy," before his brother escorted him from the theatre. Luckily, we actors never missed a beat, and my own son provided my students and me with a valuable learning opportunity.

Even the adult leaders do not always provide good examples. At one campus, I had a building supervisor who was quite nice, but who lacked good training in being an audience member. This was compounded by a leaky roof and our need to have it fixed. During semester exams — mine were always performances — he brought a contractor into my classroom and led him around on a tour of the drippy problem, pointing and whispering, while students were on our in-room stage acting. After about three minutes of noise, moving furniture, and finally a cell phone ringing, it was apparent that the actors had lost it. I sent out a hushing "shh," which seemed as unimportant as my students' need for quiet. I then called "cut," told the students to take a minute to regroup, waited for the two men to leave, and allowed the students to start over. They did great, and the whole class learned an important lesson.

Food and drinks can be both a loud and messy final act. Most theatres have signs that instruct audience members to dispose of food and drinks before entering the auditorium. The audience area is usually sloped toward the stage and the seats are tight, making cleaning difficult; besides, eating is not a quiet process. Unfortunately, there is always someone who sneaks it into the show. At one performance, we had an eater and drinker on the back row who munched and slurped loudly. After several complaints, our house manager asked him to step out into the lobby to finish, which he did, but he left his drink wedged in the folded pop-up seat. It just happened to be the seat I usually took to watch my students perform, so when I folded down the seat, the large cola fell over, making a loud spilling noise. It then proceeded to gush down the slope of the seating area until it trickled into the pit, forcing everyone in its path to put their feet in the aisles to avoid the mess. After the show, sticky cola was tracked everywhere. Since the young man was a student at our school, his parents agreed that he should be the one to clean it up, and he did.

Taking an Audience Grade

Objective: To practice audience etiquette
Target areas: Being an appreciative audience member
Performance time: Not applicable
Requirements: *Peer Evaluation*, pen or pencil, live performance of scenes or a play

- This activity can be done with any performance, both in class and during assemblies, field trips, and/or live shows. If you are lucky enough to be able to take your students to performances of live plays in your area, instruct them that their behavior will be graded from the moment they leave the bus until they board it again at the end of the field trip. You will be pleased with the results.
- In class, students will watch every performance, evaluate each quietly on paper, and support their co-actors by being quietly encouraging before and after they take the stage and watching respectfully during each scene. During performances, students will never dig through backpacks or purses, leave their seats, make faces or noises, or do anything that may be distracting to the actors. After each scene, students will take a break from evaluating their peers to clap heartily.
- Consider taking off ten or twenty points each time a student causes a disruption. Some teachers go so far as to make it a pass or fail grade (since even one disruption can affect the grades of those who are performing). Inform your students of your policy in advance.

Chapter 3

Starter Scenes

Spotlight on

Peggie Boring
Retired teacher of twenty-four years

Margaret Annette Boring, known to her friends and colleagues as Peggie, boasts a resume that makes many other teachers seem a little green. She began teaching theatre in 1977, but only after having already spent several years teaching English at the university level and developing and implementing a statewide curriculum. Over the next two and a half decades, she stayed busy enough for a half dozen teachers, taking her students to state-level competitions, writing articles, receiving a number of awards, participating in community theatre, writing and receiving grants, and then putting those awards to work to better the lives of artists, journalists, and free speakers.

Yes, the one thing for which Peggie Boring is most known in the Southeast is her passion for freedom — and she fought the fight for all theatre teachers, actors, directors, and audience members. After having taken a majority of the awards at a preliminary play competition, she and her talented students were on their way to state. The subject matter of their award-winning play was controversial, so she always made potential audience members aware in advance of its sensitive nature. Even after passing muster at competition and in the eyes of the actors' parents, her judgment eventually came into question. Her art survived a few hacks by the school principal, went to state competition without some of its lovely shadows and highlights, and still managed to place second — a feat that not many may claim to have accomplished.

In the end, however, she was demoted, a move that had a disciplinary look and feel, and the battle for teachers to have a say in choosing their curriculum began. She won her case at the Fourth Circuit Court level, so the other side appealed. The Supreme Court declined to hear their case, so it came back to the Fourth Circuit Court. In a fight that lasted seven years and withstood some extraordinary legal "magic," she lost her case by a single vote from a panel of thirteen. Still, she came out a clear winner. Peggie Boring has gathered in her corner a number of respected individuals and organizations who stand firmly in her defense. Furthermore, she has established herself as an artist of integrity and passion. Since her case, she has won numerous educational, theatre, and free speech awards.

There are few who would argue that theatre curriculum gets a lot of attention from administrators. Only a handful of districts nationwide even boast a Theatre Arts Curriculum Guide, but most have them for the core subjects. At the same time, not many even have clearly documented standards or parameters for what is acceptable and what is not (as was the case for Ms. Boring — until after the fact). Without any of these guides to restrict her, Peggie Boring made an artistic choice, and by doing so, she opened doors for the rest of us, made our ways clearer, shed light on our paths.[1]

Why would a teacher with so much experience and such a dramatic story to tell spend her time playing theatre games with teens? "Games of empowerment, bonding, and introspection bring about the true meaning of ensemble: a group of people working together for a common cause," she explains.

As an outstanding teacher, Ms. Boring uses a number of activities to get her students engaged in the bonding process. In *Near and Dear,* students are instructed to bring something "special" to class. They then sit in a circle and discuss how this object is important. She explains, "The point is to bond, introduce yourself on a personal level and learn to be cooperative, accepting, nurturing, and trusting." In a modified version of the game, students must then write a monolog that includes the item they brought either as a meaningful prop or at least mentioned. Later, of course, they will rehearse and perform the pieces.

In *Character Wars*, actors form a circle, assuming the characters from the play in which they are currently involved. This could work in a similar way if students are doing scenes rather than a play. One "character" asks

---

[1] Peggie Boring's story is told as part of a book, *Silent No More: Voices of Courage in American Schools,* edited by ReLeah Cossett Lent and Gloria Pipkin, Heinemann, 2003.

another a question, and the receiver must answer it "in character." Sample questions may include anything that would help an actor to better understand the role in which he is cast, such as, "What were you like as a child?" Other questions may help actors to understand their characters' fears, dreams, goals, and desires. After the receiver has answered his question in character, he then asks one of a different "character." This continues until all have had a chance to both ask and answer a question or until the teacher redirects. This activity is a wonderful way to start each rehearsal.

"Acting is reacting and being in the moment," Ms. Boring explains. "Improvised situations tap into each actor's creativity and inner life experiences. They learn to allow themselves to become vulnerable and express emotions in a natural manner. They put away their own 'filters' and allow the characters to express emotions as they would naturally." Put like that, it doesn't sound much like playing, does it? But ask any teen and they will say it is fun — and fun in learning is a must!

Thank you, Peggie Boring, for helping to make the art of teaching theatre clearer, freer, and more fun!

Topics for Discussion

- Are you afraid of what your peers might think about your performances? What are some things you would prefer that they said or thought? Do you think they have these same fears?

- What do you hope to learn from this class? What skills or talents do you hope to improve upon? How do you plan to apply these after leaving this class?

Introducing Scene Work

Some teachers consider scene work an exact science, and others are so flexible that introductions are optional. Whatever you choose to do in your class, do your students a big favor and let them know your exact expectations ahead of time. Just as any adult would, students feel anxiety when the instructions are vague or when the teacher does not set clear guidelines and limitations. Some things you will want to discuss with them in advance include behavior during others' scenes, how each performer should approach his or her own scene, what is allowed during the setup for each performance, whether or not you want them to drop their heads after the introduction and at the end of the scene, and the proper way to strike their sets.

> ### Acting Tips
> **Remember these basic tips when performing any scene**
>
> • **Always face the audience (if you can't see them, they can't see you!)**
> • **Remember that you don't have to go fast to have good energy; take your time and keep your energy high**
> • **Try to look confident even if you are nervous**

You may have a particular type of introduction that you really want your students to use. Perhaps you want a short introduction using only their names, their characters, the title of the scene, and the author (for monologs and duets). You may prefer the longer, more narrative introduction; it is cleverly arranged, resembling the trailer for a movie. Either one can be intimidating for a student who fears the stage or who is so focused on remembering his first line that he feels nauseated. Lessen their fears by having them do a series of short performances of just their introductions.

The following few performances assume that your actors have never done scene work, nor have they been in front of an audience. Whether this is true or not, using the starter scenes, even with advanced actors, gives you — the teacher and director — the opportunity to set the standards in your classroom. Furthermore, beginning and advanced actors will start at the same pace and be given the chance to find their footing comfortably before taking on more challenging acting assignments.

1. Just Kidding – Basic Introduction

Objective: Clarify the basic expectations of scene work
Target areas: Confidence, presentation, following directions
Prep time: 15-30 minutes
Performance time: 30 seconds each
Requirements: Chair, stage (or performance space)
Group size: All perform individually

- Instruct students that they will perform a scene called "Just Kidding" in which they are graded on everything from the moment their names are called to the moment they return to their seats.
- The performance will include approaching the stage quietly, promptly, and confidently. The student will then set up one chair (moving the chair is a requirement, preparing students for quick and quiet scene changes in future performances), walk to the front of the stage, give his introduction, assume a creative starting position for his "performance," and then drop his head (if this is the scene starter you use). After he has taken a second to "get into character," he will then dramatically act out his two-word line, "Just kidding." After his line, he will again drop his head (if this is your routine), pause, get out of character, look up appreciatively at his audience (who will, by then, be clapping), and then quietly and confidently strike his chair. He will then take his seat without making any verbal or nonverbal "remarks" about his performance. The performance will end when he is in his seat.
- Students must use a real play and its author, and they should use a character name from that piece. However, they do not need to memorize a scene.
- Consider giving perfect scores only to those students who can stay focused during the "Just kidding" line.

Example: Melissa's name is called, so she confidently stands, sets her chair where she wants it, checks the rest of the stage quickly, then approaches the audience. She stands confidently, makes sure she has their attention, then begins. "Hello, my name is Melissa Winchester, and I will be portraying Michelle from *Something about Nothing*, by Cody Kendall." She then stands behind the chair, places one hand on the back, and drops her head. After a few seconds, she lifts her head and with complete seriousness says, "Just kidding." Still serious, she drops her head, waits for the audience to clap, looks up confidently, removes her chair from the stage, and returns to her seat in the audience.

Modifications: Challenge the class to come up with unique ways to say their line, modeling it after famous moments in movies. Also, have students write dramatic or comic one-liners on index cards and substitute them for the "just kidding" line.

Allow students to do the same starter scene for a duet or group scene. How will actors be introduced? Will one person introduce all actors or will each actor take part in the introduction?

2. Just Kidding – Creative Introduction

Objective: Clarify the basic expectations of scene work
Target areas: Confidence, creative thinking, dramatic structure
Prep time: 20-30 minutes
Performance time: 1 minute each
Requirements: Chair, performance space
Group size: All perform individually

- Instruct students that they will perform a scene called "Just Kidding" in which they are graded on everything from the second their names are called to the second they return to their seats.
- The performance will include approaching the stage quietly, promptly, and confidently. The student will then set up one chair, walk to the front of the stage, give his introduction, assume a creative starting position for his "performance," and then drop his head (if this is the scene starter you use). After he has taken a second to "get into character," he will then dramatically act out his two-word line, "Just kidding." After his line, he will again drop his head (if this is your routine), pause, get out of character, look up appreciatively at his audience (who will, by then, be clapping), and then quietly and confidently strike his chair. He will then take his seat without making any verbal or nonverbal "remarks" about his performance. The performance will end when he is in his seat.
- What makes this starter scene different from the basic one is the actual content and placement of the introduction. Students will write creative introductions for their "scenes" (see example). You may want to familiarize them with the plot, the title, the author, and some of the characters from at least one play so that they do

not have to do too much reading to prepare, or, of course, they may use a movie. This should be a simple activity, not a fully memorized scene. The introduction should be memorized, but it does not have to be word for word.

• Consider giving perfect scores only to those students who can stay focused during the "Just kidding" line.

Example: Melissa's name is called, so she confidently stands, sets her chair where she wants it, checks the rest of the stage quickly, then approaches the audience. She stands confidently, makes sure she has their attention, then begins. "Michelle fears spiders more than anything in the world — well, not more than being alone, but close. After her brother accidentally locks her in the cellar, she allows her fears to get the most of her. *Something about Nothing*, by Cody Kendall." She then sits in the chair with her knees pulled up to her chest in a frightened posture and drops her head onto her knees. After a few seconds, she lifts her head and with complete serious and fright says, "Just kidding." Still serious, she drops her head, waits for the audience to clap, looks up confidently, removes her chair from the stage, and returns to her seat in the audience.

Modification: Have students do the same starter scene for a duet or group, finding creative ways to involve and introduce each actor without taking away from the scene itself.

Advanced Modification: Have students start their scene with a teaser, a small sampling of the scene, then step out of character to do an introduction. They will then step back into character and resume the scene. Because these activities are all starter scenes, do not focus too much on memorization; instead, get students comfortable taking the stage, and introduce them to a variety of ways to introduce themselves and their pieces.

Just Kidding Planning Guide

Date: _____ Name: _____

1. Just Kidding – Basic Introduction

You will perform a scene called "Just Kidding – Basic Introduction." You will be graded on everything from the moment your name is called to the moment you return to your seats. In your performance you will:

- Approach the stage quietly, promptly, and confidently.
- Set up one chair, walk to the front of the stage, give your introduction, assume a creative starting position for your "performance," and then drop your head. After you have taken a second to "get into character," you will dramatically act out your line, "Just kidding." After your line, you will again drop your head, pause, get out of character, look up appreciatively at your audience, and then quietly and confidently strike your chair.
- Then take your seat quietly. The performance will end when you are in your seat.

You will have 15 minutes to plan this activity

Find the following information in any script, and fill in the blanks.

"Hello, my name is _____, and I will be portraying the character _____, from the play _____ by _____."

Practice the line until you can say it from memory.

If your teacher has not already told you, find out the answers to the following questions:
1. May I use any greeting, or must I say "hello"? Underline your teacher's response.
2. Should I use just my first name*, first and last, or does it matter?** Underline her response.
3. What kind of eye contact should I use during the intro? What about during the "Just kidding" line?
4. What should we learn from doing this mini-scene?
5. Are we allowed to do a line or two from the script before we say, "Just kidding"?

After the Performance:

1. How do you think you did?

2. Were you nervous? Explain your reasons for your nervousness (or lack of nervousness).

3. What were some of the comments your peers made?

4. What can you do to improve before next time?

First name means the name others call you on a normal basis. Avoid nicknames unless that is the name you regularly use.
**If you are going to an audition, always use both your first and last name, even if the director knows you. This will help him to find you quickly in his stack of headshots or applications without having to clarify. Even if you think he knows you, he may not know your last name off the top of his head, or he may not be able to think of it with all the other things he is concerned with at the time.

2. Just Kidding – Creative Introduction

Now you will perform a scene called "Just Kidding – Creative Introduction." You will be graded on everything from the moment your name is called to the moment you return to your seats. In your performance you will:

• Approach the stage quietly, promptly, and confidently.
• Set up one chair, walk to the front of the stage, give your creative introduction, assume an equally creative starting position for your "performance," and then drop your head. After you have taken a second to "get into character," you will dramatically act out your line, "Just kidding." After your line, you will again drop your head, pause, get out of character, look up appreciatively at your audience, and then quietly and confidently strike your chair.
• Then take your seat quietly.
• The introduction should be memorized, but it does not have to be word for word. You may use the same script you used in the first *Just Kidding* mini-scene, or you may find a new one. It is important that you know the storyline to be able to create an introduction.

Sample Introduction: Michelle fears spiders more than anything in the world — well, not more than being alone, but close. After her brother accidentally locks her in the cellar, Michelle allows her fears to get the most of her. *Something about Nothing*, by Cody Kendall. *[Note that, in the sample, you only have to identify the play's title and author. You will not say your name. You will identify your character's name because he/she is the person about whom you are speaking.]*

To prepare for your creative Intro, do the following:
• Write a creative introduction using what you know about the play you have selected.
• Practice the introduction until you can say it from memory.
• Ask your teacher for permission first if you would like to attempt a line or two from the script before saying, "Just kidding."

You will have _____ minutes to write, memorize, and practice your creative introduction

Practice writing your creative introduction on notebook paper. When you are satisfied with the wording, write the final version below:

_____
_____
_____
_____
_____

After the Performance:

1. How do you think you did? Did you improve from last time?

2. Were you nervous? Explain your reasons for your nervousness (or lack of nervousness).

3. What were some of the comments your peers made?

4. What can you do to improve before next time?

3. The Story of My Life

Objective: Clarify the basic expectations of scene work; begin acting and developing a character before an audience
Target areas: Confidence, character, dramatic structure
Prep time: 15 minutes
Performance time: 1-3 minutes each
Requirements: Writing materials, chair, performance space
Group size: All perform individually

- Students will write an introduction for their life story as though it were a play.
- Students will present their introductions and follow them with "monologs" of their life stories. The monologs will be prepared but not written or memorized. Each should be rehearsed to last about one to two minutes. Monologs may be a summary of each student's life, the recounting of an incident, or they may even be futuristic. If students insist, allow them to use fictional events (for reasons of privacy).
- Each monolog should include a beginning, an obstacle, rising action, climax, and a clear ending.
- Students should be natural, because, after all, they are portraying themselves.

Example: Kyle's name is called, so he takes the stage, places his chair with its back to the audience, and then approaches the audience with a simple introduction. He then sits in the chair, backwards, so that he is facing the audience over its back. He drops his head, pauses, and lifts his head. Now he looks intently at a book that isn't really there, lying on a table to his right. He talks about how his mother always kept his scrapbook up to date, cut out articles in the paper about his accomplishments, and included the yearly school pictures. Then things got tough and the economy slipped. His mom had to get a job, and suddenly life seemed to fall into chaos. The book was neglected; his pictures and articles, the ones they've remembered to cut out, are in a pile underneath. He recounts the finals of the big wrestling competition last year. His mother was supposed to be there, but something happened at work and she couldn't make it. It caused a huge fight, but later that same week, his dad was laid off from his job. Kyle's mom was the sole breadwinner. What if she didn't have a job? What if she had come to the match instead of staying at work? Might she have been fired? "I realized I had been selfish and immature," Kyle continues. "Suddenly, I understood that I was living a really great life compared to my grandparents and their grandparents and that I should stop whining and start appreciating what I have, you know? I mean, I'm seventeen and my mom just had to start working when I was fourteen. A lot of kids — their moms work two jobs all their lives. I'm lucky ... really lucky." He drops his head, waits for the audience to respond, then strikes his chair and returns to his seat in the audience.

Modifications: Have students portray a relative (parent, sibling, aunt or uncle) telling about the event in the student's life rather than a first-person account. Because this is more advanced, have them do this modified scene after they have completed the basic *Story of My Life.* You might also have them tell the story of their grandparent's or parent's life in the character of that person. This is a wonderful way to explore one's family tree and history while learning the basics of acting.

Sample Scenes:
The day I was born
I used to say/do the funniest things
I'll never forget the day ...
I became a [profession] because I wanted ...
The day I got married
The day I died

Sample form

The Story of My Life Planning Guide

Date: _____ Name: _____

3. The Story of My Life
• You will write an introduction for your life story as though it were a play.
• You will present an introduction and follow it with your life story. The monolog will be prepared but not written or memorized. It should be rehearsed to last about one to two minutes. It may be a summary of your life, the recounting of an incident, or it may even be futuristic.
• A good monolog will include a beginning, an obstacle, rising action, a climax, and a clear ending.
• Be natural when performing because, after all, you are portraying yourself.

You will have _____ minutes to plan this activity

Some samples of scenes you may choose to do include:
The day I was born
I became a [profession] because I wanted …
I used to say/do the funniest things
The day I got married
I'll never forget the day …
The day I died
Or you may do another scene, but get your teacher's permission first.

What are some events in your life you think the class might find interesting? List six or more.

_____   _____
_____   _____
_____   _____

Pick the event you think will make the best monolog and brainstorm at least three subtopics to the event.

_____
_____
_____

On notebook paper, write your monolog in casual, natural language, as though you are speaking to a friend. Do not worry about the wording too much. Be sure to include your three subtopics from above. When you are satisfied with your storyline, rewrite it below.

_____
_____
_____
_____
_____
_____
_____
_____
_____
_____
_____
_____

Give your monolog a title. Identify yourself as the author, and write the title and author here.

_____

Now write a creative introduction for your monolog.

_____

_____

_____

After your introduction is written, consider the following:
• Can you identify the basic parts of a story in your monolog? Does it have a beginning, a conflict, a climax, and a well-formed ending? If not, make changes before you go any further.
• Is the story interesting? If not, make it more interesting before going any further.

When you are ready, practice saying the introduction and monolog until you are comfortable with them. They should not be memorized. Instead, it should sound natural, like you are telling a story.

After the Performance:
1. How do you think you did?

2. Were you nervous? Explain your reasons for your nervousness (or lack of nervousness).

3. What were some of the comments your peers made?

4. What can you do to improve before next time?

4. Ta-Da!

Objective: Clarify the basic expectations of scene work; begin acting believably
Target areas: Confidence, awareness, pantomime
Prep time: 5-10 minutes
Performance time: 1-2 minutes each
Requirements: Writing materials, chair, performance space
Group size: All perform individually

- Students will select a situation in which they must prepare and then enter a "space." It can be a room, an area, or an idea; it can be indoor, outdoor, or fantasy.
- For this scene, each will create an introduction that will allude to the place they are entering, but that will not give it away completely. In other words, the introduction will be like a riddle of sorts.
- The students will then create solo silent scenes in which each physically "prepares" for his entrance and then makes the entrance believably. It should be full of detail, but not so much that it is hard to follow.
- Afterward, the audience will discuss the scenes, guessing each entrance. If the actor was a success, the audience will likely guess the mystery entrance right away.

Example: After a basic introduction about everyone having to make sacrifices, Nick goes to the back of the stage (Up Center) and drops his head. When he starts the scene, it becomes apparent that he is not alone. He is being forced into the area by people on all sides. At first he struggles, but after a moment, he decides he is outnumbered and appears to comply. He tries to walk bravely, but fear is etched all over his face and body. He looks up and tries to find strength in the heavens. He looks to his left and right, seeking mercy from his captors. He looks behind him, but his captors urge him on in a way that makes him wince in pain. Very slowly and very cautiously he works his way to the "opening" between him and the audience. At the entrance, he pauses, gathers his strength, and parts the vines that separate him from the mouth of the volcano. When he sees the sputtering ash and cinders, he recoils, trying to break away, but his captors force him on. He fights them and even manages to push one of them into the volcano, which spurts up an angry ball of fire, a sign that it wants a willing sacrifice. Nick summons his strength, approaches the mouth, says a final prayer, and "falls" in. Afterward, since he is already postured with his head down, he simply pauses, then lifts his head, and takes his seat in the audience.

Sample Scenes:
A frightened actor taking the stage for his Broadway debut
The Pearly Gates
Going out into a blizzard
Your first day at a new school
A man entering the church on his wedding day
A convicted murderer entering the gas chamber
Being surprised with a party on your birthday
Meeting a blind date who is better than expected

Ta-Da! Planning Guide

Date: _____ Name: _____

4. Ta-Da!

- You will select a situation in which you must prepare and then enter a "space." It can be a room, an area, or an idea; it can be indoor, outdoor, or fantasy.
- For this scene, create an introduction that will hint at the place which you are entering, but which will not give it away completely. In other words, the introduction will be like a riddle of sorts.
- Create a solo silent scene in which you physically "prepare" for your entrance and then make the entrance believably. It should be full of detail, but not so much that it is hard to follow.
- Afterward the audience will discuss the scene, guessing your entrance. If the you were a success, the audience will likely guess the place of your entrance right away.

You will have _____ minutes to plan this activity

Some samples of scenes you may choose to do include:
  A frightened actor taking the stage for his Broadway debut
  A man entering the church on his wedding day
  The Pearly Gates
  A convicted murderer entering the gas chamber
  Going out into a blizzard
  Being surprised with a party on your birthday
  Your first day at a new school
  Meeting a blind date who is better than expected

Or you may do another scene, but get your teacher's permission first.

What are some entrances you think the class might find interesting? List six or more.

_____

_____

_____

_____

_____

_____

Pick the entrance you think will make the best scene and brainstorm things to which you could react in that place. Remember, this will be pantomime, so keep it simple.

_____   _____   _____

_____   _____   _____

_____   _____   _____

Sample form

Write the events of your silent scene briefly, identifying the basic parts of a story.

The beginning: _____

_____

_____

The conflict: _____

_____

_____

The climax: _____

_____

_____

The ending: _____

_____

_____

Give your silent scene a title.

_____

Now write a creative introduction for your scene. Write the finished version on the lines below.

_____

_____

_____

_____

After you've finished writing your introduction, consider the following:
• Is the story interesting? If not, make it more interesting before going any further.
• Can you clearly express all of the parts of your scene in pantomime? If not, simplify it.

When you are ready, practice your silent scene until you are comfortable with it.

After the Performance:
1. How do you think you did?

2. Were you nervous? Explain your reasons for your nervousness (or lack of nervousness).

3. What were some of the comments your peers made?

4. What can you do to improve before next time?

65

5. What a Mess!

Objective: Clarify the basic expectations of scene work; begin acting and moving believably; begin developing plot
Target areas: Awareness, imagery and recall, movement
Prep time: 15-20 minutes
Performance time: 2-3 minutes each
Requirements: Writing materials, performance space
Group size: All perform individually

- Students will create an imaginary room full of things. These things may be furniture or something else. However, a good scene will revolve around a theme and will stick to it.
- In the improvisation, students will enter the area, identify a "problem," and fix it. In fixing the problem, actors will have to move in and around a series of obstacles in an overly crowded room. Things can hang from the ceiling, stick out of walls, or be piled on top of one another. They can be stationary, on rollers, or motorized. These can be left in place (in which case actors will have to remember to crawl over or under them each time they encounter them) or they can be moved (in which case actors will show size, weight, shape, texture, and mobility).
- After the "problem" has been fixed, students will wrap up the scene with a solid ending.

Example: Antonia takes the stage, gives a simple introduction about needing a quiet place to "escape," and then crosses up left and drops her head. When she lifts her head, she is very quiet, like one who does not want to be found. She "slinks along an invisible wall," rounds a corner mysteriously, and slips into a dark room. She closes the door behind her, locks it, secures the deadbolt, and searches frantically for the light. She finds it, looks around, and when she is sure it is safe, she takes something from her pocket and places it in a safe spot up high. She then takes a number of measures to further secure the door, including pushing something large and heavy up against it, nailing it shut, and running tape across it. When she feels completely safe, she returns to that item she had placed up high and takes a moment to appreciate it. She rubs it against her face, smells it, feels it, and hugs it. She then removes its imaginary wrapper, takes a chewy bite, and sinks lovingly to the floor to enjoy the rest of her candy bar before dropping her head to end the scene. She then lifts her head, stands, and returns to her seat.

Things to consider should include:
How large is the area?
How does it smell, what is the air like, and how clean is it?
What is in the area?
What is the "problem"?
What is the solution?
Why are you fixing the problem?
How difficult is the resolution?
What is the "pay off"?

Modifications: This may be done as either a silent scene or with speaking. Add another dimension and have students pair up for the scene. An introduction for this scene is optional.

Advanced Modifications: Make the activity even more challenging by having students add an obstacle they are not likely to encounter. For example, have them do their scenes as though wading through thick Jello, in slow motion (or as though weightless), or with a swarm of bees buzzing about.

Sample Scenes:
Changing the light bulb in a dark barn full of live animals
Entering and exiting through opposite sides of a room full of lab
    spiders in tanks when some are blocking the exit
Cleaning up after a party you were not supposed to have as your
    parents return home
Building an igloo in a snow storm
Rearranging the furniture in your apartment to make it look more
    impressive

What a Mess! Planning Guide

Date: _____ Name: _____

5. What a Mess!

- You will create an imaginary room full of things. These things may be furniture or something else. However, a good scene will revolve around a theme.
- In the improvisation, you will enter the area, identify a "problem," and fix it. In fixing the problem, you will have to move in and around a series of obstacles in an overly crowded room. Things can hang from the ceiling, stick out of walls, or be piled on top of one another. They can be stationary, on rollers, or motorized. These can be left in place (in which case you will have to remember to crawl over or under them each time you encounter them) or they can be moved (in which case you will show size, weight, shape, texture, and mobility).
- After the "problem" has been fixed, wrap up the scene with a solid ending.

You will have _____ minutes to plan this activity

Some samples of scenes you may choose to do include:

Changing the light bulb in a dark barn full of live animals
Entering and exiting through opposite sides of a room full of lab spiders in tanks when some are blocking the exit
Cleaning up after a party you were not supposed to have as your parents return home
Building an igloo in a snow storm
Rearranging the furniture in your apartment to make it look more impressive

Or you may do another scene, but get your teacher's permission first.

What are some messy places you think the class might find interesting? List four or more. Circle your final choice.

_____

_____

_____

_____

Answer the following questions.

1. How large is the area? _____

2. How does it smell, what is the air like, and how clean is it? _____

_____

3. What is in the area? _____

_____

4. What is the "problem"? _____

5. What is the solution? _____

6. Why are you fixing the problem? _____

7. How difficult is the resolution? _____

8. What is the "pay off"? _____

Draw a floor plan of your messy area. Include the things in the room that contribute to its being messy. Using map pencils or markers, make a key and color code the following obstructions:

❑ Things on the floor   ❑ Things on the walls   ❑ Things on the ceiling

Use a dotted line to show your path through the mess. If you go under an item, mark it with a U. If you go over an item, mark it with an O.

Give your silent scene a title.

_____

Now write a creative introduction for your scene. Write the final version below.

_____

_____

_____

_____

After you finish writing your introduction, consider the following.

• Is the scene interesting? If not, make it more interesting before going any further.
• Are you allowed to talk? If not, use plenty of pantomimed detail to express clearly the items with which you are working.

When you are ready, practice your scene until you are comfortable with it.

After the Performance:
1. How do you think you did?

2. What were some of the comments your peers made?

3. What can you do to improve before next time?

Chapter 4

Exercises

Levi Curtis

Spotlight on Lamaline, New Foundland and Labrador

Levi Curtis is not your ordinary theatre teacher, nor does he live an ordinary life. He lives in Lamaline, New Foundland and Labrador, the seventh largest island in the world. Known for its fishing, one would not think that theatre would have much of a chance, but the arts are huge there, and very well appreciated. Mr. Curtis brags, "There are so many repertory theatres on our island that one would have to travel by car for a week just to get from tip to tip if they chose to stop at each one along the way."

He would know. He stays busy teaching at not just one or two schools in the area, but a total of a half-dozen. On top of that, he is a professional actor, and he works behind the scenes making films. His students compete in the Canadian Improv Games and are also active in The International Thespian Society, and of course, they stay busy producing plays, too. All of this means Mr. Curtis fills his schedule making sure they are well supervised.

Despite a busy schedule, he finds plenty of time for creativity in the classroom. There is always some activity to help students overcome an acting dilemma or to reach a new height. For concentration, he plays *Concentration Circle*. Students stand in a circle, shoulder to shoulder, and they take three steps back. There is no speaking, gesturing, or using eye contact to send nonverbal messages. Using instinct only, students must step back into their original positions one at a time. If more than one moves at the same time, they must start over again, back at the shoulder-to-shoulder position. They play a version of *The Bridge* to develop teamwork, and if he feels that students need to increase their sensitivity to a handicap or other physical condition, they find a way to mimic it — not just for a short while, but for an entire school day. For example, he once had average-weight students pad themselves to become seemingly overweight so that they could experience what it was like to be heavy.

"One of my favorite activities," he boasts, "is a trust exercise I do with them. We use the gym for an afternoon because it's wide open and has lines marked on the floor. Students use the lines to get from point A to point B. Once they are there, I tell them to close their eyes and find their way back to point A." He goes on to say that even after they have mastered the activity, he changes things up a bit by putting obstacles in their paths, having them run, or having them do the activity while walking backward. This increases their awareness of their surroundings, and it also increases their sensitivities to sounds, smells, feelings, instincts, and others around them. You will find a similar activity, *Pioneers*, later in this chapter.

Despite his cool nature, there are things that Mr. Curtis dislikes about improvisation and spontaneous acting. "I don't like the stereotypes that kids will often use as a crutch." He explains that when he was putting together an improv team for The Canadian Improv Games, the actors started getting campy and acting stereotypically gay. "I stopped them and we had a talk about the harmfulness of certain stereotypes. They started talking about their fears regarding homosexuals." Most will agree that fears drive young people to bully and make fun of those they do not understand.

It was during this discussion about fears that one of the boys in the group found the courage to say, "That's me. You're talking about me." He was admitting that he was homosexual. This had to be a difficult thing for him to admit, especially in light of the stereotyped characterization he had just witnessed. It probably was not easy for his friends, either, but despite his fears that they would abandon him, they all stayed close. Mr. Curtis recounts that even though he disliked the course the activity had taken, after he redirected them, the results were undeniably positive. In the end, the group became much more sensitive to reality and avoided stereotypes. "The beauty of theatre," he adds, "is watching kids gain self-esteem, self-confidence, and to see the wonder of who they are."

Yes, Mr. Curtis, you are right. And the beauty of a great educator —

71

and you are great — is being a responsible and spectacular tour guide in your students' adventures, making sure every moment is valuable, and never allowing misdirected efforts to stay off the healthy path.

Topics for Discussion

• Athletes and dancers warm their muscles with stretching and massage prior to putting strain on them. Actors warm up, too. What are some ways that you think actors prepare to take the stage?

• Do you remember playing "pretend" as a child? Why did you play? What benefits did you get from it? Was it fun? If you were told to play "pretend" today, would you be successful? Explain.

• Why do you think many athletes and pop stars can successfully become actors, but few actors break into professional sports or music? Can acting be learned? Why is the acting business so competitive?

Introduction to Exercises

Exercises are activities intended to target specific areas, much like physical exercising targets particular muscle groups. Actors have many tools that must be fine-tuned in order to be considered truly great. These tools include the way they move their bodies; the many ways they manipulate their voices, not only so that the sounds are interesting, but also so that they may be heard; and the way they use pauses, interpret the script, and apply inflection to words and sentences. There are many, many more tools, and for each tool, there are numerous activities that can be used to sharpen them. Entire books could be written about all the different acting exercises, so obviously only a few of those exercises may be mentioned here.

Before we discuss the tools, ask yourself, "Why do actors perform? What is their purpose?" Actors are messengers. Unlike the man in the truck who brings you a package, however, the actor brings you his message with emotion, style, mood, and character. His main objectives — that is, if you are to receive the message — are to be seen and heard.

No matter how believable the emotion or how talented the actor, if the audience cannot see his face and clearly interpret his movements and if they continually strain to hear him, they will not understand the message.

Earlier in this book, you read that actors should try to face the audience by maintaining a one-quarter or full-front stance when possible. This is only one of the ways to be seen by the audience. Actors are also responsible for wearing their hair and positioning hats so that they do not block facial expressions or prevent the lights from illuminating their faces. These are very mechanical objectives; in other words, they have little to do with the artistry of acting. The actor must simply remember to do them. However, an inexperienced actor might look as though he is "trying to be seen" while a good actor finds a way to perform the same mechanics in such a way that the audience never realizes he has done anything special. The difference is that the latter actor practiced over and over and over again. He exercised various tools of his craft until performing them became second nature. He makes it look effortless.

Acting Tools

Voice

Perhaps the most complex of all actors' tools is the voice. As you also learned earlier in this book, there is more to having a great voice that just being heard. Truly talented actors have mastered varying their voices' *pitch* so that they never sound monotone (unless, of course, they have a monotone character) or so that their voices have a more interesting quality. Pitch mastery also allows actors to relay the message more effectively, portray a wider variety of characters, and make each character unique.

Besides pitch, the ability to *project* one's voice so that it may be heard in all parts of the audience is also important. Sometimes when you are listening to the radio, you are in the mood to hear the music softly and other times you want it to be loud enough to rattle the walls, so you reach for the volume button. But have you ever turned it down low enough that you could hear parts of the song but other parts seemed to fade to nothing? Or perhaps you had it so loud that it ruined the mood of a particular song. Characters and their situations — like songs — require that the actors playing them be able to access their own personal volume buttons. Of course, actors don't have the luxury of a literal button. Instead, they must learn to strengthen and use their *diaphragms* (the muscle that forces air from the lungs) to project sound, even when speaking in a stage whisper. Each actor must interepret the script and know enough about his character and the situation to understand what level of volume will work best. There is no way to teach those subtle nuances in a book; they are learned by studying and working with good directors for a long time. However, you can learn to project your voice, and with time and practice, the rest will soon follow.

Articulation is another vocal quality that, when mastered, will help each actor to clearly deliver his message. To *articulate* is to vocalize every necessary sound in every word clearly. It does not mean to give every letter a sound. Good articulation means knowing when certain sounds can be clipped without sounding mushy, too. For example, words with "t" sounds in the middle, such as "letter," "better," and "little," need a compromised sound in order to be believable. If you hold a feather in front of your mouth and hit the "t" sound fully, the feather will move from the burst of breath behind the sound. In some dialects, this strong "t" sound is completely normal, but in American English, we tend to clip it just a bit. Be careful; you don't want it to sound like a "d" as in "ledder." You simply want to eliminate the strong burst of air behind the "t," making the sound almost like a "t" and "d" combined. At the same time, the "er" sound at the end of the word can be tricky, too, especially if you are from the deep South or the Northeast.

The best way to appreciate good speech easily is to listen to people who make livings with their voices. These people may be voice actors (like cartoon voice-over artists), disc jockeys, newscasters, public speakers, preachers, actors, singers, or even teachers. What you will notice is that, even though they can be heard, they are not all perfect. Some use slang, questionable grammar, or have pronounced dialects. Not long ago, most speakers worked hard to lose their dialects, but today this is less of an issue. A speaker's accent makes him unique. Furthermore, being too perfect can make a speaker "less attainable" to his audience who want to hear someone more natural. He must not be so proper that he sounds "hoity toity," and he must not be so casual that he sounds colloquial. He must find a balance and become comfortable using widely socially acceptable speaking patterns.

Of course, acting is very different from those professions mentioned above. Unlike a newscaster or a DJ, an actor is rarely cast in a role where he may relax and be himself. Usually, he is playing a character — someone different from himself. The best actors, therefore, are those who can sound like a street-wise gang member, a college professor, an English nobleman, a Russian musician, a child, or a cartoon mouse. In a word, a good actor must be diverse.

When you are working on a scene, record your voice and listen to the recording. Make notes about your voice, and use the notes to make improvements. Consider taking a voice or speech class, and ask others to give you feedback. Sometimes we are so used to the way our voices sound, we need someone who is less familiar with us to point out where we can use improvement.

There are a number of other factors to consider when preparing your voice for the stage. *Quality* is the pleasantness of one's voice and can include pitch, volume, and articulation, but it can also be affected by many other things. Some people have deep, resonating voices while others have squeaky or high-pitched. Some voices have a lovely, musical quality, and some sound rough or stressed. Just as every laugh is different, so is every voice. Not all of these voices are considered pleasant, either. Some of the most recognizable voices in film belong to actors who were told that they would never make it because their voices were all wrong. Can you think of some people whose less-than-prefect speaking voices catapulted them to fame?

Movement

The next big tool with which an actor must learn to work is his own body and the way it moves. *Movement* classes teach actors to work with every muscle in their bodies so that they can move like animals, fire, a candlestick, or whatever the script — or their interpretation of it — calls for. This is where young and inexperienced actors tend to become self-conscious. Since I first started teaching with games, I have read many messages on my students' faces that told of fears or worries they never said with their voices. The way a girl crosses her arms might mean, "I am too tall and skinny for this activity. Everyone will look at me. I will feel vulnerable." The way a boy acts goofy when the scene calls for him being serious is his way of saying, "I would prefer everyone laugh at me for trying to be stupid than for trying to be serious but looking stupid anyway." Some actors are so afraid of how they will look that they clam up or only give a small percentage of what they are really capable of. Start slow, and when your students have exhibited some confidence, increase the movement.

Again, a set of encyclopedias could be written on just movement exercises, but obviously, for the sake of this book, only a few of these activities can be included. However, many of the games in the other chapters will also help actors to become better movers. Refer to the *Target Areas Index* for a full listing.

Other Tools

Some of the less obvious and more difficult acting skills to master include learning the finer points of timing, developing strong and unique characters, maintaining realism and believability, learning to focus and concentrate (also known as becoming absorbed in the moment), developing a strong sense of teamwork and family, and so many more.

Use the exercises in this chapter as well as some of the games and other activities to fine-tune your young actors' skills. Remember to save the games, exercises, and activities you learn at conventions and seminars.

6. Relaxation

Objective: Focus and concentration
Target areas: Listening, relaxation, breathing control, imagery and recall
Performance time: 10-20 minutes
Requirements: Spacious area
Group size: Whole-group activity

- Have students lie on their backs with their hands down by their sides. They should not cross their legs or arms, nor should they bend or prop up their legs. They will close their eyes and relax their jaws. It will help if you dim the lights.
- This works well with soft music playing in the background to drown out erroneous noises and to set a mood.
- Explain to students that this is just about visualization and concentration; it is not hypnosis (as many students jokingly call it). They should listen to the audio cues and experience in their imaginations the situation being read.
- Read one of the following stories to the relaxed group. Your voice should be soft and soothing. Circulate among the students as you read. Make sure they are relaxed by gently lifting their wrist an inch or two off the ground and letting go. They should not try to control the fall. If they are sleeping, this will also cue them to stay awake and focused on the activity.
- After they have "experienced" the entire story, have them sit up and discuss the questions below the activity.

Story One – Flying

Close your eyes and relax. Imagine you are lying on a cloud a mile above the earth. It is cool here, but not too cold. Feel the coolness spread over your arms and legs as clouds cover the sun above. Relax. Now there is a tiny break in the clouds, just enough to let a little ray of sunshine warm your brow. Feel the warmth. Your arms and legs are cool but your head is toasty and warm. Now let that ray of sunlight get bigger until it warms you all the way from your head to your fingertips and toes. Now imagine that the cloud upon which you lie is cottony soft. Your back sinks into it. You can feel it cup your head and your hands. If you pinched a little off with your fingers, it would be softer than silk, almost like warm oil slipping through your fingers. But you don't pinch any off, because it is cradling you like a baby, keeping you comfortable and relaxed. What sounds do the clouds make? Can you hear a gentle breeze? Can you hear the gentle rumble of a distant thunder? It's not a scary sound. No. It's comforting, like hearing your grandma's heart beating when she gives you a long, loving hug.

Now imagine that you are lying face down in the same cloud, snuggling into its softness, like warm water, only you can still breathe. Below, you can hear the birds as they fly in small flocks over the earth. You can hear the high-pitched, sweet call of the swallow, and in the distance, a flock of wood ducks. You can't bear not to be flying on such a beautiful day, so you let go of the cloud and allow yourself to float downward. As you slowly fall, the cool air passes by your face and ears, fluttering loudly. This isn't a helpless fall. You aren't in trouble. You are flying like the birds, and you feel free. Below you, the earth is a mass of blue, green, and brown. You can see the sea to one side and the mountains to another. Pick one. Where will your adventures take you today? The sea or the mountains? As you fly, the sun heats your back and the wind cools your face. As you head to your destination, the other gets farther and farther behind you. Smell the air! Can you smell it? Feel the freedom as the air rushes past you. Ride the waves of the air currents as they take you up and down over the landscape.

As you get closer, you descend a bit to explore the landscape below. What do you see? What kinds of shadows and movement animate the ground? Quickly, take inventory of your surroundings because the sun is going down, and soon it will be dark. You've been flying so long now the sun is almost to the horizon. Above you, the first evening star twinkles. It's getting cooler now, and time to wind down your journey. Where will you sleep tonight? What is comfort to you?

You can fly, so you can go anywhere. Where will you go to rest for the evening? The sun is down now and the stars are filling the sky. Before you land, take one last swoop upwards into the night sky. Higher. Higher. Good. Now let your imagination do the landing. As you sail through the darkness to approach your destination below, allow your imagination to take over the landing. Watch as you settle for a peaceful and relaxing end to your flying adventure.

Instruct students to slowly come to a sitting position, and discuss the following questions.

Discussion Questions:
- Where did you go, the sea or mountains? Why?
- What did you smell when you got there?
- What did you see below you?
- Describe your landing.
- Were you a bird, human, or something else?
- What did you like most about the activity? The least?
- How can an actor use the activity to help him with his craft?

Note: Actors' abilities to recall images, dreams, and visions clearly from their own imaginations can be valuable tools. On stage, they can conjure these images when needed so that they may realistically and naturally react to them. Someone who has eaten ice cream and can recall the memory has a much better chance of reacting to it on stage in pantomime than someone who has never had the pleasure of really eating the food. Remind students that imagery and recall can be practiced.

Story Two – Colors
Close your eyes and relax. Imagine you are swimming in a pool made up of your favorite color, but it's thick and warm, like paint. Feel the color around you. Above your head is complete darkness, space, a void. You are not afraid. You are completely and totally relaxed. If you stop swimming, you will not sink. Your color will support you. Scoop up a handful of the colored liquid and toss it. As it flies through the air, it changes. It becomes a butterfly and flutters away rather than falling back to earth. You pick up more handfuls of the liquid and toss them, and again, more butterflies. You continue this until the air above you is thick with butterflies of your favorite color. At first they flutter about in chaos, but then they begin to fall into place, like delicately flowing lines of

music. If you listen closely you can hear them, you can hear the music and you can see it. The butterfly music swirls around you, gently embracing you, lifting you from the pool of color until you are suspended above it. The music wraps around your legs, your arms, your body with a softness and purity not found on earth. Then you feel solid ground under your feet. Below you, you can still see that welcoming pool of color, and the butterflies are still fluttering in the distance, so you dive, an expertly perfect dive into the pool of color below. As you descend into the depths of the color, you feel it envelop your body and rush past you. Then you surface. The ripples of the color work their way outward. Above your head, darkness and blackness turn to an artist's clean white canvas. Each of your fingers is a tube of color. Your index finger on your right hand is the color of anger. Point it at the canvas in bold, angry movements. The index finger on your left hand is peace. Use it to soften the angry strokes you made earlier. Now see what colors and emotions your other fingers have to offer. Create a painting in your mind to reflect the colors in your palette and the emotions in your heart. First your right hand. Point. Now your left hand. Now step back and look. Do you like the painting? What would happen if you smeared that part there with your hand? You reach for the painting, but instead of touching a canvas, the painting absorbs you. You fall into it. Remember the colors? They are all around you instead of in front of you. They are above you, behind you, to the left and right. What does red feel like if you touch it? How does blue taste? Can you lay your head on green? The colors are swirling faster and faster, they are becoming more intense, they are spinning around your body, your head, your feet like a tornado. Suddenly, this violent rush of colors ejects you. You are thrown from the painting, back into the original pool of your favorite color. You lie there, comfortable, relaxed. What temperature is this color? What texture is it? What does it smell like?

Instruct students to slowly come to a sitting position, and discuss the following questions.

Discussion Questions:
- What was your favorite color?
- What music did you hear?
- What color did you see as anger?
- What color was peace?
- What patterns or designs did you make with anger and then peace?

- How did these colors look, feel, taste, smell, and sound?
- What did you like most about the activity? The least?
- How can an actor use the activity to help him with his craft?

7. Vocal Warm-up

Objective: To prepare the voice for performing
Target areas: Listening, breathing control, voice
Performance time: 3 minutes each poem
Requirements: Poems
Group size: All participate

- Distribute copies of the poem you plan to use. It is best that students memorize the selection if you plan to use the same one over and over again. Memorization is recommended because it will save time in the future. Furthermore, it will free students' hands, allowing them to assume a more speaker-friendly posture.
- Have students stand in "perfect posture," feet directly under their shoulders, arms loosely by their sides, chin parallel to the ground, knees slightly bent, shoulders back and relaxed, and spine straight. While they will not always be able to assume this position while in character, it is the preferred posture for warming up the voice as it allows actors to speak from the diaphragm. This is a relaxed posture, not stiff; nor should it be uncomfortable.
- Use a variety of teacher-led voices, pitches, styles, volumes, and dialects to recite the poem. A few are listed for you, but as always, be creative.
  - ~ Start low in pitch and work your way up the scale. Stop when you cannot comfortably go any higher. Rejoin the group when they work their way back down the scale to a level you can realistically master without stressing your vocal cords.
  - ~ Spread out in the acting space and take turns projecting until each actor says he can hear each of the other actors without missing a sound.
  - ~ Try to say the poem as many times as you can in one breath. Try to beat your record each time.
  - ~ Learn the proper dialect for the poem for the show on which you are working. For example, if you are playing Kate Keller from William Gibson's *The Miracle Worker*,

learn to say the poem in a Southern accent. If you are Annie Sullivan, say it with an Irish dialect.

~ Overarticulate all of the sounds of each word in the poem.

~ Say the poem in a stage whisper, but loud enough to be heard in the back row.

~ Say the poem with various emotions.

• Use the poem in conjunction with customized lines that specifically target trouble spots in your show. For example, if you are doing *The Miracle Worker*, but the word "miracle" sounds more like "meercle," include a sentence from the script containing that word or create your own clever reminder, such as, "We will arrange miniature maroon marigolds in marvelous arrangements in reward for our mastery of the word miracle, miracle, miracle." It's a mouthful, but when your students have learned to say it clearly, you may relax. Not only will they remember it for years to come, they will never again say "meercle."

The Actor's Prayer

Here go I to the spotlight, the footlights, the stage.
Give me the strength and courage to perform
Without inhibition.
May I think not of myself,
But of my team and my audience.
May I remember my teachings,
Reach new heights, tread new paths.
Guide my voice, body, heart, and mind.
Lead me to understand, interpret, and express.
Here go I, an entertainer,
Into the spotlight, into the footlights, onto the stage.

The Ultimate Tongue Twister

A nonsensical poem,
To get your mouth goin'
As fast as your brain
While staying precise.
If you mess up,
Start over again,
And keep going till you get it right!

Sassafras simple,
Pumpernickel dimple,
Alluicious Alfonzo's glass albatross eye.

Six silly synonyms,
Exactly eight antonyms,
A loquaciously long-legged, short-sighted fly.

Three hundred hyperboles,   [pronounced hi pur´ bu lees]
One groom and a bride-to-be,
They're really a couple of amorous spies.

A half dozen digital,
Decidedly fidgetal,
Mathematical, fanatical guys.

Stop!
Stop the top before it drops
And plops upon the purple pop
And makes a glop of gooey slop
On Papa's favorite flopping spot!

8. Samurai Warrior

Objective: Explore need for controlled
movement, following directions, trust, and
teamwork on stage; work with exaggerated
stage combat and facial expressions

*Nick and Cody practice
self-control in a game of
Samurai Warrior.*

Target areas: Stage combat, movement, self-control

Performance time: 5 minutes each scene
Requirements: Performance space
Group size: 2 actors per scene

• Two students play at a time. Instruct students that the back side of
each of their forearms is a weapon. It is the only part of their bodies
that is invulnerable (that cannot be hurt). They will engage in a
slow-motion martial arts battle, but any time any nonweapon part
of either student's body touches the other's weapon, they must
respond appropriately.

- Actors may also use their legs, but again, it must be in slow motion. The other player must be able to see all "attacks" coming so that he may safely react without risking injury to himself or the attacker.
- Both actors may attack and block with their forearms. The goal is to perform the battle in slow motion, keeping all motion fluid; secondarily, students may attempt to create a plot, but not at the expense of the cooperation and movement. If teamwork is used, students will create an interesting visual and both will be successful (even if one does lose the battle).
- Add this to any improv scene without prior notice, or drop it into the middle of rehearsal when movement is suffering.
- Give bonus points to students who use stage combat movements you have taught them in class — only if they have used them correctly and with the proper safety measures in place.
- Encourage huge displays of pain and suffering when a student is "struck" with another's weapon (after all, this is acting!).
- Furthermore, encourage students *not* to compete to see who can "win" but to see who can best follow the directions.
- Limit players to three strikes; a player receiving three strikes against him must die a dramatic death.
- Remind actors that falling in slow motion will be the true test of their self-control.
- Set this game to Japanese music and have students create a "Samurai Warrior" scene with a beginning, rising action, climax, and clear ending.
- Study kabuki and use this game as both a reward for the studying and to teach larger-than-life movement.

9. Taking a Walk

Objective: Explore basics of movement, including posture, gestures, facial expression, and exaggerated movement; imagery recall and pantomime.
Target areas: Creative thinking, movement, pantomime
Prep time: 5-10 minutes*
Performance time: 1-2 minutes each
Requirements: 3-5 index cards and a marker for each student, performance space
Group size: All perform individually

*Use the *Generic Activity Planning Guide* on page 26 or the guide for activities 4 or 5 if desired.

• On index cards or similarly sized pieces of paper, have students write two or three things they might find in the woods, in the desert, in a plush hotel room, in a prison, and so on in large words, one per card. Specify two or three environments, and provide several cards for each. Group the environment cards, but keep the various environment groups separate from one another.
• Gather all the cards for the various environments, and select one set. Randomly place eight to ten cards throughout the room, and select one student to take a walk through it. As he approaches each card, he must respond appropriately.
• Start with just a walk, but then add this to improvisation situations, such as "You parachuted out of an airplane, but instead of your intended target, you landed here. Use pantomime and improvisation to indicate where you should have landed versus where you actually landed."
• Place some cards under others so that both can be seen, such as putting a "snake" under a "log." Encourage the student to find ways to respond to both cards.
• Save cards from previous years or classes, and with your new group, have them guess the environment in which the student is taking his walk.
• Let two or three students take a walk together, giving their story a beginning, rising action, climax, and a clear ending.

Example: Manal is taking a walk through the woods. Her teacher has placed a number of cards from her pile for the woods about the room. Manal knows she is "in the woods," so her walk begins the moment she takes the stage. She looks lost and frightened. She reads the first card and returns it to its location. Then she hears something. She hides behind the spot where another card has been placed; obviously this one is a tree or bush. She watches as the thing from the first card comes in. We can see by her face that it is very frightening, but as it comes closer, she lets us know it is also quite smelly. After the "bear" leaves, Manal continues her journey, careful not to step in "what the bear left behind." Oops! She read the card with "big rock" written on it, but too late. She tripped over it and twisted her ankle. Luckily there is a "stick" card nearby. She can use that as a cane until she finds her way out of the woods. Wait! What's this? A "cell phone" card? Someone must have lost their phone in the woods. She opens the phone and dials. It still works! "911? Hi. My evil stepmother tried to lose me in the woods. Can you send help? Hurry, please, before Papa Bear comes back!"

Sample Environments:
The desert
The moon
An expensive jewelry store
A prison
A farmers' market
A ship two hundred years ago
Prehistoric times with dinosaurs

10. Near and Dear

Casey creates a monolog using an item that is dear to her.

Objective: Getting to know one another, bonding, and expression
Target areas: Getting to know you, trust
Performance time: Varies per individual
Requirements: Students bring special item from home, space for discussion circle
Group size: All participate

- Each student will bring to class an item from home that they hold "near and dear" to their hearts.
- In a circle, each will take a moment to present his item, tell its history, why it is important, how he honors it (its special place and treatment at home), how he feels about the object, and what he plans to do with it in the future.
- The teacher and other students can assist with questions or comments.

Modifications: After the initial group presentation, have students write a one- to two-minute monolog (additional preparation time will be needed after the initial activitiy). The object may be the subject of the piece or it may simply inspire it. For example, a toy won at the fair may remind a girl of her first date and how the evening ended when the boy won this prize for her. Try to keep the activity as free of rules and restrictions as possible. Encourage students to include anything in their presentations that they want, including music, a song, a dance, or whatever they feel would best help to express the feelings, sounds, sights, smells, tastes, and textures of the object.

11. Honey, I Love You

Objective: Practice focus amid forced distraction; utilize creative and strategic thinking
Target areas: Getting to know you, creative thinking, strategic thinking
Performance time: About 20 minutes
Requirements: Large space
Group size: Whole-group activity

- Have the class make a standing circle with one person in the middle.
- The person in the middle (A) approaches someone in the outer ring (B) and says, "Honey, I love you. If you love me, smile."
- B must respond, "Honey, I love you, but I just can't smile." If he does not smile, the person in the middle finds someone else and repeats the process. If B does smile, he goes to the middle and A takes his place in the circle and the game continues.
- The object of this game for all B's is to avoid smiling so as to never end up in the middle. However, A has a different objective — to get a B to smile so that they may switch places. If the person in the middle is having difficulty getting someone to smile, help him or her with strategies.
- Instruct students to approach people who have not been in the middle unless they are having difficulty.

Modifications: With reluctant players, add a competitive component. Allow them to send students out of the circle who have either been to the middle twice or who try to get five people to smile and fail in a single round. The last two students standing can have a stare-off, a smile-off, or a one-legged hop-off.

Try a speechless version of this game in which the person in the middle must hold his classmates' stares. Any person in the outer ring who either breaks his gaze or breaks a grin must take his place.

12. Find Me!

Objective: Develop sense of family; rid students of inhibitions regarding touching
Target areas: Getting to know you, trust, awareness
Performance time: About 20 minutes
Requirements: Large space
Group size: Group activity in pairs

Bianca and Melissa using their sense of touch in a game of Find Me!

• Pair students off.
• Have the pairs stand together, and give each a couple of minutes to observe the other's hands without touching them. They may ask their partner questions about their hands.
• Closing their eyes, students will mix up and get in a circle, holding hands; you may have to corral some strays. Pick one student to go to the middle, keeping his eyes closed; the rest may now open their eyes. Have the one in the middle feel his way around the hands in the circle until he has found his partner's hands based on what he thinks they feel like. Once he has successfully done this, mix the students up again, picking a new student for the middle. Continue doing this until everyone has had a chance to find their partner.
• You can make the game harder by having them put their rings in their pockets. Also, for braver students, have them do the same activity feeling faces.

Modifications: Have the students stay mixed up and keep their eyes closed while trying to find their partners in the jumble. For this version, remind them that remaining quiet is very important if the activity is to work.

Put the class in a circle and use a stopwatch to see how many students each can name in one minute with his or her eyes closed.

Have students sing the ABC song in unison, but while attempting to pick out their partners' voices from among the crowd.

13. Huggie Bear

Objective: Develop quiet sense of teamwork; solve problems without being able to discuss them
Target areas: Getting to know you, awareness, timing, dressing the stage (modified version)
Performance time: About 5 minutes
Requirements: Large space
Group size: Whole-group activity

Mr. Morrow participates with the students in a game of Huggie Bear.

- Gather all of the students into an area, perhaps the stage, and say "Huggie Bear" and a number. For example, "Huggie Bear, six!"
- Students must make groups of six and give a large-group hug. After you have counted them, say "Huggie Bear" and a new number. Again, they must reorganize into groups of the number you have called. There are some fun modifications to this game with endless potential.
- Use numbers from one to the number present in the group.
- Students who cannot form a group of the number called should make a group of "remainders." You can require them to make "sad bear faces" if you want.

Modifications: Play *Huggie Bear Family Reunion*; in this version, students make groups of the goal number, but they pose for Huggie Bear family pictures instead of just hugging. You may take pictures of the groups, but it is not necessary. The goal is an added benefit of practicing dressing the stage, so allowing students to see the outcome of their "family pictures" would be a bonus.

Issue challenges, such as hugging with their ears or wading through Jello to get to their groups. It will be fun to see how quickly they can get through the Jello when they see another attempting to get the final spot in the group.

Huggie Bear *provided by Bill Klipstine, Live Oak High School, Morgan Hill, CA.*

14. Junk Yard Drill Team

Objective: Learn precision and cooperation needed for group drill activities; appreciate benefits of listening, creativity, and teamwork needed for stage, especially musical theatre

Students use racquets to practice timing and teamwork in Junk Yard Drill Team.

Target areas: Teamwork, timing, movement, presentation
Prep time: 2-3 class days
Performance time: About 5 minutes per group
Requirements: Several similar items per group, performance space
Group size: Large groups

- Students will gather several of the same item. For example, they will find as many crutches, telephones, clipboards, binders, bandanas, toy lawn mowers, wagons, rulers, place settings of flatware, or canes as they can. The items need to be either the exact same size, shape, weight, and color, or they need to make a pattern (such as two small, two medium, and two large, or all pastel).
- Assign students to groups according to their item. Each group will create a drill team routine with these things (much like the rifle squad in the military). These are not dances, but dancing is allowed only as support to the drill routine, not as the main focus.
- The performance should be creative, larger than life, and it should demonstrate a high level of teamwork and precision. Timing is very important. Students should explore sound, movement, eye contact, facial expressions, and even dramatic structure when choreographing their routine. Additionally, they should attempt to include theme, mood, and even plot. However, they should not let plot become the overriding focus. The object is to exercise as many of the dramatic elements as possible while maintaining teamwork, creativity, and precision.
- Due to the amount of preparation required to perform this activity successfully, consider giving it the same "weight" in your gradebook as a memorized scene.

Modification: Challenge students to work with the freeze element, during which part of the group will stand "frozen" as another part works on, then, without warning, the "frozen" students will join in. A similar theatrical device is used in a number of modern plays.

Sample Drill Team Items: Gather items that create a nice visual or audio pattern. For example, a number of umbrellas will look and sound nice together despite their colors, as will scarves. On the other hand, it will be difficult to do a routine with twelve different rulers if half are mismatched and cannot do the same things as the others. Take time to discuss the characteristics of the items you are considering. Look in your prop room, or talk about things most people already have at home. Ask yourself, "How can we make this more interesting?" For example, rather than bringing just a phone handset, bring the cord, too, so that part of your routine can be a rodeo-style phone round-up, complete with cord lassos! The following items are usually easy to find and will do nicely:

- Rulers
- Umbrellas
- Beverage cans or bottles (be careful with them; you may want to use uncarbonated products if the drink is still in them)
- Scarves
- Cell phones
- Musical instruments
- Makeup items
- Pots, pans, and wooden spoons

Junk Yard Drill Team Planning Guide

Name: _____ Date: _____

14. Junk Yard Drill Team

- Gather several of the same item. For example, find as many crutches, telephones, clipboards, binders, bandanas, toy lawn mowers, wagons, rulers, place settings of flatware, or canes as you can. They need to be either the exact same size, shape, weight, and color, or they need to make a pattern (such as two small, two medium, and two large, or all pastel).
- Your group will have all of the same items, and you may have more than one set of items. Each group will create a drill team routine with these things (much like the rifle squad in the military). These are not dances, but dancing is allowed only as support to the drill routine, not as the main focus.
- The performance should be creative, larger than life, and it should demonstrate a high level of teamwork and precision. Timing is very important. You should explore sound, movement, eye contact, facial expressions, and even dramatic structure when choreographing your routine. Additionally, attempt to include theme, mood, and even plot. However, do not let plot become the overriding focus. The object is to exercise as many of the dramatic elements as possible while maintaining teamwork, creativity, and precision.

You will have _____ minutes to plan this activity

How many people are in your group? _____ You will need that same number of items. What are some items your group can gather? Circle your final choices and set a date for students to bring them.

_____ _____ _____
_____ _____ _____
_____ _____ _____

Bring items by _____ (Share phone numbers if a reminder phone call is needed.)

Tell basically what will happen in your drill routine. This is the plot. After you know the basic idea, you can plan the choreography. If needed, write the movements on notebook paper. They do not have to be turned in to your teacher.

_____
_____
_____

After writing the drill routine, consider the following.
- Is the above scene interesting? If not, make it more interesting before going any further.
- Are you allowed to talk? If not, use plenty of pantomimed detail to clearly express your message.
- When you are ready, *practice your drill routine until it is precise.* Refer back to your story often to make sure you are not straying from it.

Give your scene a title.

_____

Now write a creative introduction for your scene. Write the final version below.

_____
_____
_____

After the Performance:

1. How do you think you did?

2. What were some of the comments your peers made?

3. What can you do to improve before next time?

91

15. Character Wars

Objective: Explore depths of characters, their relationships with other characters and those who share the scene with them
Target areas: Instincts, character, self-control
Performance time: Varies
Requirements: Space for discussion circle
Group size: Whole-group activity

- This activity works best with a play cast as rehearsal enhancement.
- Position students in a circle and instruct them to be in character from the time they enter the circle to the time they leave. At no time may students drop character.
- Select one student to start. He or she, in character, will ask a question of another character. This person must answer the question in character using his knowledge of the script, the author, the history of the play, and his own deductive reasoning. The two may work through the question and the answer until both are satisfied that it has been thoroughly resolved.
- The person to whom the initial question was asked may now ask a question of another in the circle. This continues until all have both asked and answered at least one question. The teacher may allow it to continue or may adjourn the session until another day.

Modification: Have students ask questions for which there is no basis in the script, forcing students to reach deeper into their own understanding of the character to answer. In these cases, they may make denials, rationalize, or make educated assumptions, but they should not recreate the history of the character (which would undoubtedly lead them to misunderstand the character).

Character Wars *contributed by Peggie Boring, Lincolnton, NC.*

16. The Middle Man

Objective: Learn to listen to and differentiate between two conversations
Target areas: Focus, listening
Performance time: 3-5 minutes per group
Requirements: None
Group size: 3 players per group

Casey listens as Inass and Alexia discuss two different subjects with her at the same time.

- Three players participate at a time. Place the three players in a triangle facing each other or in a line (with the listener in the middle). Assign one person to be the listener and two people to be talkers.
- The two talkers will both speak to the listener as though he or she is the only other person, ignoring the other talker. The talkers must continue their parts of the conversation even if the listener gets confused. The listener must try to participate actively in both conversations.
- Encourage talkers to ask open-ended questions and to be satisfied only with a full reply. This will force your listener to converse with the two talkers rather than simply listening on the surface.
- Place conversation topics in a bowl to help students (or to challenge them).
- Buzz out students who fail to continue to engage in coversation.
- Alternate positions so that each student gets his turn in the middle.

Modifications: After one group of three has demonstrated the activity successfully, the rest of the class can break into groups of three and work simultaneously. Challenge the talkers to talk about completely opposing things, such as "I love math" and "I hate math."

17. Sit, Stand, and Bend

Objective: Deal spontaneously with forced physical stimuli in a scene
Target areas: Awareness, strategic thinking, movement
Performance time: 5 minutes per group
Requirements: Chair, performance space
Group size: 3 players per group

In a game of Sit, Stand, and Bend, *a doctor and his assistant treat a man for a foot ailment.*

- Three players play this game at a time, and there should be one chair on stage.
- The teacher gives the three players a scene to improvise, and at all times during the scene, one player must be sitting down, one player must be standing, and one player must be bending over.
- Each player must effectively express his reason for the movement. For example, the bending player might be picking something up or have a crick in his back. The standing player might be waving at someone off in the distance. When a player changes to one of the other positions, the others must adjust as well.
- This is a difficult scene, and wrap-up is even harder, so praise those who come up with effective conclusions!
- Despite the seemingly competitive nature of this activity, encourage students to work together. There is a strong desire in games like this to try to talk over one another. Remind them to listen, react, share the stage, and work as a team toward a common goal.

Modifications: The bending actor may also squat, lie, kneel, or anything else that puts him on a lower level.

18. The Bridge

Objective: Use teamwork and strategic thinking to move about the room and overcome obstacles
Target areas: Teamwork, strategic thinking, following directions, self-control
Performance time: About 20 minutes
Requirements: Large space, almost as many chairs as students (or newspapers for younger students)
Group size: 7 students per group

• Divide your students into several teams of about seven each.
• Each team will need almost as many chairs (or sturdy cubes) as they have students. Provide one team with one fewer chair, one with two fewer, and so on. It will make the game more interesting if each team has different obstacles.
• Put your teams in different parts of the rooms, and tell them to work their way "over there." Point to some other place in the room.
• They may not step on the floor. They may only use the cubes or chairs, their minds, and their bodies.
• Instruct students not to talk. Tell them that if they talk, you will remove one of their chairs and give it to the quietest team. While this sounds like punishment, it actually makes the game more fun (and challenging). Also, by not allowing them to talk, you are forcing them to establish leadership roles, to work more cooperatively, and to use nonverbal methods of communication.
• Throughout the process, place obstacles in their way, forcing them to find ways to go over, under, through, and around.

Modifications: The first time you do this activity with your class, tell students they may not talk but they may communicate nonverbally. The second time, mix up your groups and allow them to talk. Compare the results. How does communication allow us to function with more ease?

If students are mastering the activity too quickly, take away a chair or cube or place more obstacles in their way.

For younger students, use sheets of newspaper (in case they fall).

The Bridge *contributed by Larry Wisdom, Van High School, Van, TX.*

19. Evolution

Objective: Students "compete" to see who will evolve into modern man first, exploring potential paths along the way
Target areas: Instincts, creative thinking, movement
Performance time: About 20 minutes
Requirements: Large space
Group size: Whole-group activity

Melissa and Cody (as fish and bird) evolve slowly in a wacky game of Evolution.

- Students mingle as single-celled beings until the teacher says "evolve." At that time, they turn to the student-amoeba closest to them and play "Rock, Paper, Scissors." Whoever wins becomes a simple animal or insect (let them have fun finding different ways to characterize this).
- Again, they will mingle, and when the teacher calls "evolve," they will again battle to see who will evolve to the next level.
- If several students make it to the most advanced level at the same time, they will battle among themselves to see who wins. However, do not allow them to stop characterizing their advancements. Challenge them to become kings, monsters, or gods. It is fun to see how progress lends itself to regression when power plays its part.
- For the basic game, the levels are amoeba, then simple animal, then advanced animal, then caveman, then modern man.
- When playing "Rock, Paper, Scissors," rock crushes scissors but not paper, scissors cut paper but not rock, and paper covers rock but not scissors.

Modifications: Rather than having students "evolve," which can cause some students discomfort due to their religious beliefs, call the game "Promotion" and have students battle to see who will become president of the company. Or call it "King of the World," and have students fight for the throne. For each, have students identify about five levels, such as mailroom worker, intern, assistant, vice president, and president or beggar, peasant, landlord, mayor, and king.

20. Electricity

Objective: Get used to working closely with peers; learn how to handle appropriate touching; build energy
Target areas: Creative thinking, energy, movement
Performance time: 5 minutes
Requirements: Space for a circle
Group size: Whole-group activity

- Have students stand in a circle. One person starts by acting like electricity is entering his body from any point in a nonpainful, energizing way. He must show it going from the entry point through his entire body to an exit point.
- Wherever it exits, he will connect to another student who will take in the electricity and repeat the process.
- Encourage students not to copy their peers, not to be afraid to touch, and to only touch appropriately.
- Celebrate creativity. Each student will have a different interpretation of electricity, and none is wrong.

Modifications: Try other visualizations, such as passing knowledge, warmth, or happiness. Slow the activity down or speed it up as you see fit.

21. Passing the Whoosh

Objective: Introduce students to a large set of objectives over a graduated period of time
Target areas: Focus, eye contact, energy, following directions
Performance time: 10-15 minutes
Requirements: Space for a circle
Group size: Whole-group activity

Alexia "whoas" Casey's whoosh.

- Because a "whoosh" is like a breeze of energy, the movement associated with it is like a "parting of the waters" gesture. Hold your hands at waist level, palms together, but fingers away from the body. Quickly move your hands away from your body, then open them and push them away from one another.

- Have students stand in a circle with plenty of room between them. Using eye contact, they will start by passing the whoosh with both the above movement and the word "Whooooossshhh" to either their right or left. This continues for a few rounds until the teacher is confident that eye contact is being used.

Alexia "zaps" the whoosh.

- Next, add the "Whoa" element. This is punctuated by holding up both hands, signifying, "Whoa! That whoosh isn't welcomed here!" At that, the person passing the whoosh must pass it the other way. You may want to limit students to one "Whoa" per round.
- After a few "Whoas" have gone around, and if the teacher is still confident that eye contact is being used, she may add "Zaps." "Zaps," accompanied by a point of the finger, send the whoosh to someone other that an immediate neighbor. The receiver may then send it to either of her neighbors, but of course, as a whoosh.
- Another fun element is the "I'm feeling the groove" move. When students can whoosh, whoa, and zap in a controlled way using eye contact, they may dance any kind of appropriate dance for as long as it takes them to say, "I'm feeling the groove, oh yeah!" The others in the circle mimic the dance, and at the end, the student with the whoosh (and of course, the groove), passes it with either a whoosh or a zap.

Students add their own element with a wild "freak out."

- A "freak out" sends everyone scrambling noisily to a new place in the circle; the player who called "freak out" begins the game again when everyone is situated.
- If a student passes it without making eye contact first, the whoosh will die. It can only be sent with the appropriate verbal cues accompanied with solid eye contact.

Modifications: Allow students to create new ways to pass the whoosh. What cue might put them into slow motion? How could you signal students to stand on one leg?

Passing the Whoosh *contributed by Jason Kruger, James W. Martin High School, Arlington, TX.*

98

22. Frames

Dr. Len Radin works with students in a game of Frames.

Photo by Darlene Radin

Objective: Explore setting mood, creating an effective stage picture, and teamwork
Target areas: Instincts, creative thinking, energy, dressing the stage
Performance time: 1-2 minutes each round
Requirements: Chair(s), performance space
Group size: 4-7 players per round

- One student takes the stage and assumes any position, then freezes (a chair may be used by any student who wishes).
- Instruct onlookers to observe the first student before moving. Does his position give them any ideas? Do they see the beginnings of a large picture? Prior to taking the stage, the next student should begin to see a theme forming.
- When a student feels drawn to join in, he should take the stage without raising his hand. This activity works best when done with only the teacher talking, (minimally) and when actors join in voluntarily.
- Limit each picture to four to six students. After the last has joined in, prompt the audience to "title" the picture, or if they do not think the picture works, to change it.

Modifications: Try the activity first without any prompts. However, you can also do the same activity by cuing them with a single word. Some examples of these might be courage, fear, loss, victory, defeat, triumph, perseverance, or joy. Challenge students to create a box of prompts for the future. This is a close relative of the *Headlines* activity.

Frames contributed by Jason Kruger, James W. Martin High School, Arlington, TX.

23. I Am!

Objective: Create feeling of unity amoung large group of students; promote confidence; utilize spare time
Target areas: Confidence, getting to know you, stage fright
Performance time: 5-10 minutes
Requirements: None
Group size: Whole-group activity, any size

• This activity can work with twenty to several thousand participants. It works extremely well with very large audiences to fill big gaps of time.
• One person leads. This person says "I am ..." and follows with a true end to his statement. For example, "I am an Aquarius." Everyone in the audience who is also an Aquarius stands and shouts, "I am an Aquarius." The leader starts with obvious things that appeal to a large group, and can then start narrowing it down to some things that are not so common.
• Statements do not have to be limited to "I am" statements. They could include "I like ...," "I feel ...," "I have ...," or anything that could be made into a short statement. However, avoid statements made in the negative, such as "I hate ...," "I have never ...," and so on. They tend to reduce the level of participation and can lead to statements like, "I hate waiting." This can have the reverse effect of what you were seeking in an activity.
• Allow the audience to lead, especially if you are using a microphone, by having members make statements for the rest of the audience to mimic.
• Throw the audience some curves by saying statements you know cannot be true for any of them (just to see if they are really listening), like "I am a green frog."

I Am! *contributed by Dr. Len Radin, Drury High School, North Adams, MA.*

24. A Perfect 10

Objective: Increase sensitivity to team members and the rhythm of the group; develop instinct
Target areas: Teamwork, instincts, listening, self-control
Performance time: Varies
Requirements: None
Group size: Whole-group activity

- This activity works best with between five and fifteen people. Unfortunately, it is the type of activity that usually works only one time. After that, it becomes too easy to plan strategies and try to beat the system. Because the idea is to build instinct, players must "feel" and listen rather than plan and strategize.
- Tell students to close their eyes and listen. They should open their eyes at no point in the activity. Tell them it would be like cheating.
- Instruct them to count from one to ten, taking turns saying the numbers. If more that one person talks or says a number at the same time, they will have to start over. It is the teacher's job to listen carefully, and if you hear two people speaking at the same time or see them signaling to one another (or peeking), say, "Start over."
- A student may say more than one number during the course of the game. Numbers must be said in the correct order, and no more than one student may speak at a time. Students should not develop a pattern (such as going in a circle) as this defeats the purpose of the activity.
- Because this game is about listening, feeling, and relying on instincts, discuss with them afterward the subtle benefits of the activity. What did you hear? Was there a leader? How did you finally accomplish the task? How can actors use this kind of instinct on stage? Why is it important for actors to establish leadership roles, listening skills, rhythms, and instincts on stage?

Sample Activity:
    Student 1: One
    Student 2: Two
    Students 3 and 4: Three
    Teacher: Start over.
    Student 2: One

Student 3: Two
Student 5: Three
Students 1, 2, and 4: Four
Teacher: Start over.

(This will continue until students have counted to ten without any two or more students speaking at the same time.)

A Perfect 10 *contributed by eighth grader Douglas Reed.*

25. Concentration Circle

Objective: Increase sensitivity to team members and the rhythm of the group; develop instinct
Target areas: Teamwork, instincts, awareness, timing
Performance time: Varies
Requirements: Large space
Group size: 8-12 students per round

- This activity works best with between ten and fifteen people. Have students stand in a circle, shoulder to shoulder. They will then take three steps back, keeping their hands down by their sides.
- Without speaking, gesturing, or using any kind of nonverbal communication or eye contact, students must take turns stepping forward until all are back in their original position, shoulder to shoulder. If any two or more students move at the same time, they must all start over.

Concentration Circle *contributed by Levi Curtis, St. Joseph's Academy, Lamaline, New Foundland and Labrador.*

26. Pioneers

Objective: Establish trust; increase sensitivity to one's movements, surroundings, and obstacles
Target areas: Instincts, awareness, movement
Performance time: Varies
Requirements: Chalk, yarn, or tape*; large space
Group size: Whole-group activity
*Do this activity indoors using yarn or tape.

Cody and Bianca walk their paths in Pioneers.

- Find a large, empty space where the ground or floor is relatively flat. This activity will not work well in grass.
- Give each student a ball of yarn (or you may use rolls of tape or bits of sidewalk chalk). Instruct them to mark off a path about twenty to thirty steps long. Their paths may cross others' paths.
- Do not allow them to straighten the yarn if it gets kinked. This will be important later in the activity.
- After they have created the paths, instruct them to stand on one end or the other. This is the designated beginning of their path. Have them walk the path beginning to end and then end to beginning several times, taking note of every move they must make.
- After they have memorized their paths, try the various activities below with them, reminding them to keep in mind what they have already discovered as they advance to the next challenge:
    ~ Have students walk the path again while keeping their eyes up.
    ~ Instruct students to attempt to get to the other end of their path with their eyes closed (you may want to have half the class act as guides for the other half and then switch).
    ~ Discuss rhythm, and then challenge actors to discover a suitable one for the shape of their path. Have them walk it again in response to this prompt.
    ~ Challenge students to consider the mood or personality of their path — is it dangerous, dreamy, anxious, or uncertain? Have them walk it again in response to this prompt.
    ~ What kind of character would walk this path? What circumstance would place him here? Where would he be going to or coming from? Have them walk it again in response to this prompt.

103

~ Have them imagine coming upon the path by accident. What might have caused it? Who might have tread here before? Have them walk it again in response to this prompt.

~ Instruct students to perform some simple business any time their path is kinked, twisted, messy, or broken (if using tape). Now have them walk the path again in response to the prompt.

~ Have students "greet" any other student they meet along their paths with a nonverbal greeting.

~ Allow students to try others' paths.

~ As you watch the students, add obstacles or challenges to individuals' journeys that you think will increase learning. For example, If you see someone whose journey appears sneaky, tell them that at that bend in the path, they hear a noise and must respond.

~ Additional prompts may include adding a line of dialog at the beginning or end of the path, encouraging a change in posture, or introducing circumstances that would change a character's mood or outlook.

• Consider adding music at some point or having students hum a theme song in character as they walk their path.

• At this point, allow students to discuss their findings and add additional enrichment ideas of their own.

27. Headlines

Objective: Create stage pictures to express mood and feel of headlines from current newspapers
Target areas: Imagery and recall, creative thinking, dressing the stage
Performance time: 2 minutes per pose
Requirements: Recent newspaper, performance space
Group size: All play in groups of 3-5

• Divide the class into groups of three to five, and position them throughout the space so that they each have their own "performance" space.

• Without showing them the pictures accompanying each story, read a headline, and tell students they have about three minutes to discuss the picture and to create it. Students will position

themselves as though they are the subjects of the actual photograph in the paper under that headline. They will freeze in this position until the teacher instructs them to relax.
- If you can, take pictures of the groups before having them unfreeze. If not, have all but one group relax, and have them observe the group still frozen. Discuss the picture and what makes it work or not work, then have another group resume its position. Do this with all the groups until they have each been observed and discussed.
- This is a valuable lesson for dressing the stage, forcing focus, and using stage pictures to express a message. The greatest value from the lesson will come from your class's discussion.

Suggestion: Take pictures of the groups and make a bulletin board displaying the pictures and headlines. Enhance the activity by having students post their feelings and observations about the activity.

28. The Hot Air Balloon

Objective: Control and understand breathing so that actors gain awareness of its function in acting and scene work
Target areas: Awareness, breathing control, voice, following directions
Performance time: 5 minutes
Requirements: Large space
Group size: All play in pairs

- Students will stand and face a partner with their hands hanging loosely at their sides and their shoulders back (not stiff, just in good posture). Their knees should be directly under their shoulders, and their chins should be parallel to the ground. (This will be referred to again as "perfect posture.") Instruct your students to take a slow, natural breath in through their nose and let it out naturally and slowly through their mouth. Did they see their partner's shoulders move? Probably a tiny bit because when the lungs fill, the expansion of the chest cavity will cause some slight movement. If their partner's shoulders appeared to move too much, as though the shoulder muscles were involved, they should inform their partner and try again until both partners are satisfied.

- Now have students place one hand on their diaphragm (the muscle that pushes air out of the lungs.) It is between the stomach and the rib cage. Tell them to press in slightly and repeat the natural breath. Not much should happen except that they should be able to feel a little tightening of the muscle.
- With their hands over their diaphragms, have students take a slow, deep breath through their nose while counting to ten. Have them hold for ten seconds and then release through their mouths over the same ten count. This time they should have really felt some tightening of the diaphragm muscle. Next, tell students to find some space away from their partner and the others. With their feet shoulder width apart, they should drop the top parts of their body over so that they are bent at the hips — not the waist. Their arms and head should hang with no muscle control, and their knees should be slightly bent. Ask them to imagine they are a hot air balloon, sagging to the ground. Now, repeat the slow breathing activity above minus the hand on the diaphragm. As their lungs fill with air, their body starts filling, too. Like a hot air balloon, they will fill from the base (their waists) up to the tips of their fingers — all in ten seconds. Then have them reverse the process while exhaling. Encourage them to keep the body thoroughly involved in the activity. (For variation, try the balloon activity for longer and/or shorter periods of time.)
- Instruct students to assume the "perfect posture" described above. Moving only their mouths (and the muscles around their mouths, they must say "he / he / ha / ha / ho / ho / huh." Each syllable gets its own small breath (note the breath mark: /), and the entire line should be done in about three seconds. The last syllable, "huh," gets a thrust (like a punch in the stomach would sound). Start very shallow and unvoiced. Continue to "breathe" the line, getting deeper each time until the students are as loud as they can be without voicing the syllables. Now add a quiet voice (a stage whisper), then a louder voice, and so on, until they are as loud as they can be without yelling.

29. The Mirror

Objective: To mimic partner's movement
Target areas: Awareness, eye contact, timing, movement
Performance time: 5 minutes
Requirements: Large space
Group size: All play in pairs

- In groups of two, each will stand facing his partner. Decide who will be A and who will be B. A will start by slowly moving as though looking into a mirror while B duplicates the movement as though he is the mirror. After about a minute, switch.
- Eye contact and timing are very important. Even when a student cannot possibly be looking at his partner, he must be aware of his movements. Discuss how this can be done.

Modifications: Have one person lead while the entire class mirrors him.

Have students plan a nonverbal scene using the mirror game based on waking up, getting ready for a date, or some other mirror situation. Perform it for the class.

Chapter 5

Games

Dan Morrow
Wilson Middle School
Speech and Theatre
Plano, Texas

Spotlight on

Dan Morrow lives the life many theatre teachers dream about. He teaches by day at Wilson Middle School in Plano, Texas, where he is involved in two very active programs: speech and theatre. Together, he and his wife, the lovely Mary Ann Morrow, own a dance and drama studio. They met while both were performing in *You Can't Take It With You,* and they haven't stopped acting in the almost twenty years since. Besides producing shows for young people at the studio, the two take turns participating in professional and community theatre so that one is always able to stay home with their two children. Sure, it's a lot to juggle, but when it is your passion, you find a way.

"I have always loved performing. I grew up listening to comedy albums my dad had (Bob Newhart, Jonathon Winters, George Carlin), and I liked the way they created characters," Mr. Morrow explains. He started performing in plays in junior high and continued through high school, and then on into college. It was at this time that he realized that teaching theatre offered him the financial stability and the freedom to still pursue his own acting, and he loved working with young people.

Most actors will tell you that they were inspired by someone — someone who made them feel special or told them they were gifted. With Mr. Morrow, he found his inspiration in — well, in a play! "Before that, I liked theatre, but it wasn't my main thing," he says of playing Dr. Carrasco, the villain in *Man of La Mancha* — not once, but twice. "It was the first musical I was ever involved with. I was really moved by the story and the character of Don Quixote." After that, he says, theatre became his biggest passion.

For a teacher who finds inspiration in characters, it is easy to see why he is such a fan of characterization games. "I like games in which actors have to portray a variety of characters in different situations. Improvisational games are the ones which seem to get actors to 'come out of their shells' and 'show off' with the rest of the group." Teaching in middle school, this is understandable, as there is so much pressure to fit into a mold. He continues, "But some really good actors aren't great at improvisation. I am very careful to make sure that they know that they don't have to be great at improvisation to be a talented actor."

The truth is, improvisation skills can be taught, and an actor's abilities can be grown. One way to do this is to find games at which they can be a success. Mr. Morrow enjoys the *ABC Game*, in which characters build a conversation around the letters of the alphabet. The audience gives two actors character types, a situation, and a random letter. They must start a scene using that letter, and as each character responds to the

> **What is your greatest gaming pet peeve?**
>
> **Mr. Morrow:** I try to teach actors to work as a team and to go with the flow of the scene rather than against it. When one actor denies what the other says in the improvisation, everything stops. But when the actors stay in the affirmative, the scene is funnier and is allowed to continue smoothly.

other, the first word of the response must begin with the next letter of the alphabet. One reason many actors excel at this game is because the focus (and their nervous energy) is almost accidentally misdirected to the letter, rather than the acting, as they work their way back through to the starting letter. They don't think about how they look, if they are being too silly for their friends' approval, and if they are "fitting in." Instead, they focus on their letters.

Another of his favorites, closely related to the *ABC Game*, is the *Question Game*. In this activity, the class is divided into two teams. The first person from each team takes center stage and is given a character and a common situation. They "compete" to see who can last the longest performing the scene in questions only. If an actor uses a statement or repeats a question, he sits out and the next member of his team replaces him. The object is to keep your team from using all its players, but since the fun is in playing, it can also be in losing, so there are really no winners or losers in this game.

As a speech teacher, too, Mr. Morrow says games have a place in the more structured curriculum as well. Of course, because the goals are different, so are the games. He enjoys setting up scenarios for the students in which they must successfully communicate a solution, carry on polite and meaningful conversations, or complete an effective job interview. Even though they appear to be playing, they are learning and having fun at the same time. In the end, the experience will be of more value to them. They will retain the information because they actually had the experience rather than reading about it or hearing their teacher tell them about it.

Dan Morrow is a wonderful example of the saying, "Teachers touch lives. They never know where their influence stops." Because of Mr. Morrow, there are many people in the world who are better speakers and more confident actors, even if their places are not in the spotlight. Many will become teachers and pass on to their students what he taught them, and so on, and so on …

Topics for Discussion

- Have you ever had a series of items to learn, so you or your teacher put the list to music? What did you have to learn? How long ago was that? Do you still remember the series? Why did it help to put it to music?

- When you study for a difficult test or assignment, what is your best learning style? Remember, your "favorite" is not always your "best." Do you learn better with music or complete silence? Do you study better alone or in groups? Do you prefer memorizing facts or trying to understand cause and effect? Why is knowing your learning style important? How can games affect that?

- Are you competitive? Do you like to win? How does this affect your school work? How might this apply to your acting?

Introduction to Games

Games help actors to improve their skills, but in these activities, students either compete against one another to try to be the best or funniest, or work together to complete a difficult task. Either way, there is a spirit of competitiveness in games that is not quite as prevalent in improvisation, exercises, or pantomimes and mimes. Many young people do not like to participate in games for this very reason. And many educational experts believe, too, that competition in the classroom hinders learning or results in a poor self-image. However, for every person who rallys against this style of learning, there are ten who recognize and tap into its benefits.

Regarding students who are reluctant to play, most will eventually participate. If you find that the competitive nature of theatre games alienates some of your students, start by trying to find out what causes their reservations. They may feel that they are being compared to their classmates. Perhaps they do not think they can be successful and that they are setting themselves up for failure. Assure them that in learning games, everyone who can take with them a bit more knowledge or improve their skills even a little is a winner. At the same time, be extremely supportive and encouraging. Let your class know that good sportsmanship is a must. After all, how can we ever make learning fun for all if some are made to feel like losers?

I have also found that playing the games with my students lets them know that I expect nothing of them that I am not willing to endure myself. I clearly relate the benefits of the game, what I hope that they will learn, and how they will be able to apply their learning In their lives and on stage. Once they know that there is a point to the activity, they will relax and have fun. And, once they have fun, their learning is limitless.

It may also help to hold discussions about the desired results and benefits of the activity either beforehand or immediately afterward. In most cases, the students will grasp your objectives without your guidance. However, I have learned that my desired objective may not be as important as their self-discovery. Often, they have an insight into the lesson that I overlooked. It is for this reason that I hold discussions afterward; I do not want to inhibit their learning by implying in advance that there may be limits. Leave the learning open and the it will be limitless.

They may feel some reassurance in knowing that there really are very few theatre games in which students compete against each other.

In most cases, students compete for completion; that is to say, they compete as a team to get to the end. In some cases, two teams may compete against one another, but in the spirit of learning, most make all finishers feel like winners. Most theatre games simply allow the actor to compete against his personal best. With the support of his class and his teammates, each is encouraged to do better than he did the last time he tried. The games have no winners or losers, but all who participate are challenged, and all who try and who remain willing learners are winners.

Again, play these games with your students and lead by example. Your participation will be the main motivator in getting your reluctant learner to see that there is nothing to fear and a great deal to gain.

30. The Three Energies

Objective: Use a variety of motivators to increase students' energy, decrease performance anxiety, and promote creativity
Target areas: Confidence, energy, movement, timing
Performance time: 5-10 minutes per round
Requirements: Space for a circle
Group size: Whole-group activity

- Place students in a circle with plenty of space between each.
- For the first energy, the **Energy Clap,** one person starts by turning to his neighbor and clapping, slowly and with eye contact. The neighbor must clap at the same time (to receive the energy) and then turn to his other neighbor to pass the clap. This continues, slowly and deliberately, several times around the circle. The object of this round is to pass the energy steadily around the circle so that both the passing and receiving clap are so synchronized that they sound like a single clap. Remember, everyone will clap twice: once on one side (to receive), and then once on the other (to pass).
- After the actors have successfully passed the clap, they will advance to the second energy, the **Energy Domino.** One person starts by making a short, quick movement, which will then be interpreted by each person in the group one at a time, starting with the person to his left. When it gets back to the first person, he will do the same movement again. However, the person to his left will create a new one, which will then move around the circle and back through him. In other words, each person will make a contribution, watch it go around the circle clockwise, and do it a second time;

then the next will start a fresh, new movement. This will repeat until everyone has contributed a new movement for all to interpret.
- After each person has contributed and it is again the first person's turn to start the round, he will now make only a sound. His sound will work its way around the circle, interpreted by the others, the same way the movements did in the last round. Everyone will do the same.
- For the third phase of Energy Domino, each student will pair up his movement and his sound while adding energy and drama. Again, all will interpret and each will have a turn to contribute.
- For the final energy, the **Energy Blast**, one person will start by doing a sound and a movement, and everyone will interpret at the same time. This is much faster than the first two energies, and it requires students to think quickly. If a student doesn't know what to do and says, "Oh! It's my turn?" the others must follow with, "Oh! It's my turn?" Do not allow any time for "thinking."
- With the Energy Blast, students can really think big and bold, explore energy through silence, or challenge their peers to reach new heights. Have fun with this one. It's a blast!

Modifications for Energy Domino

For advanced actors (or after students have successfully completed the above three phases of this energy), allow them to play the round with both sound and movement from the start. Challenge them to play by beats (one beat or syllable for combined sound and movement — for example, pointing and saying "Go!" — two beats or syllables for the next round — for instance, jumping backward and saying "Watch it!" — and so on). After they have completed the primary rounds, remove some of the rules and allow them to use popular phrases, dance moves, and more. This will help them to build confidence moving and vocalizing in front of their peers.

When students are getting to know one another, play the game with names. Each student must do a movement and a phrase, but the phrase must contain his or her name. This will help them to get to know one another, especially as the phrase with each actor's name is passed around the entire classroom of students.

If you are playing this game with a play cast, allow them to use key words or lines (their own or others') from the play. This is a super way to see how others interpret or inflect lines differently.

31. The Backwards Selling Game

Objective: Sellers seek and use audience clues to sell a product they know nothing about but of which the audience is fully aware
Target areas: Awareness, listening, creative thinking, strategic thinking
Performance time: 10 minutes per round
Requirements: None
Group size: One seller, all participate

- In this game, the audience knows what the host is selling, but the host does not.
- The student selected to be the host steps out of the room while the audience decides on a product. The product should be dual faceted. In other words, instead of selling "tomatoes," sell "rotten tomatoes."
- The host returns and tries to sell the product using generic references to size, shape, and function. However, as the audience cues him (or as he calls on them), he will begin to see his product taking shape.
- When he is able to call his product by its actual name, the audience claps, signaling that he has won. At that point, he must wrap up his scene.

Sample Products:
Dead flashlight batteries
Automatic room cleaner
Homework Buddy Robot
Automatic Answering Pen for school tests
Year-old Halloween candy
Substitute teacher remote control

32. Kitty Wants a Corner

Objective: Increase awareness, eye contact, nonverbal communication, and energy
Target areas: Instincts, eye contact/nonverbals, energy
Performance time: As long as desired
Requirements: Space for a circle
Group size: Whole-group activity

- Have the class stand in a circle with one player in the middle playing the kitty. The kitty approaches his classmates and says, "Kitty wants a corner." They reply, "Go see my neighbor."
- While the kitty's back is to the others, they will make eye contact with each other, communicating nonverbally a desire to change spots with them. The kitty has to try to beat one of them to his spot, putting that person in the middle.
- Use spiking tape to mark spots to avoid confusion.
- This game can go on endlessly, so it's a good time-filler when you have a few minutes to spare at the end of the period.

Modification: Allow the student in the middle to choose any animal, perhaps "Grizzly bear wants a cave," but he must become a bear as he seeks his cave. Those wishing to change spots must also move like bears. This will become more interesting as they try to race to spots while still being animal-like. If the racer breaks character to move, place him in the middle.

Kitty Wants a Corner *contributed by students of Lake Highlands High School, Dallas, TX (2000-2001).*

33. Snake Tag

Objective: Build strength while cooperatively strategizing; develop teamwork and energy
Target areas: Teamwork, strategic thinking, energy
Performance time: 5 minutes per round
Requirements: Large space
Group size: Whole-group activity

Casey and her crew tag Nick in Snake Tag.

- One person starts by trying to tag another.
- When anyone else is tagged, he links up to the original tagger, forming a short chain, and they try to tag more.
- Eventually, the linked taggers will form a long chain and can encircle their prey.
- The last person to be tagged wins, but he starts the next game as the tagger.

Modifications: For a variation on the game, have the tagger close his eyes (be sure to move furniture and other hazards out of the way). Each additional link in the chain must also close his eyes. This causes the game to become more multisensory.

Switch and have the tagger keep his eyes open while the prey keep theirs closed. After they are tagged, they may open their eyes to join the chain.

34. Bang!

Objective: Last person standing wins
Target areas: Focus, eye contact, listening, timing, self-control
Performance time: 15 minutes per round
Requirements: Space for a circle
Group size: Whole-group activity

Students use listening skills and fast reactions to play a game of Bang!

- Have the class stand in a circle with one player in the middle (A). The person in the middle will make a gun with his thumb and forefinger. He will turn to the others, one at a time, and point and say "Bang!" Each of those who are "shot" (B) will duck down all the way to the floor, and the two people still standing to either side (C & D) will turn to one another and say "Bang!" in an "old-West" style shootout.
- The object is to be first to say "Bang!," however, besides being fast, you must also be keen. There are several ways to get out, including:
  - ~ Not ducking if you are the one (B) to whom the person in the middle said "Bang!"
  - ~ Saying "Bang!" to the person to your right or left (C or D) before the person between you (B) has ducked
  - ~ Being the last to say "Bang!" in a shootout
  - ~ Saying "Bang!" when you aren't supposed to
- As long as B ducks when A "shoots" him, he stays in. Of the other two having the shootout (C & D), the one to say "Bang!" first will also stay in (as long as B has ducked).
- The person in the middle judges the shootout, and there can be ties. To be "out" means to "die" where you are.
- The last two players left from the circle will stand back to back. The

person who was in the middle names a category and begins listing things in that category. As he says each one, the two players take one step out. When he says something that doesn't fit, the two turn and duel. The faster shooter wins and starts the next game.

Bianca and Melissa have a shootout at the end of the game.

Modifications: For a nonweapon version of the game, play Bunny. In this version, guns are replaced with bunny ears and the word "bang" is replaced with "bunny." Instead of shooting, A aims bunny ears at B, B puts his hands up to make two bunny ears, and the people to either side (C & D) rush to his side to put up one ear, the one with the hand farthest from B. While this version is molded more toward younger audiences, it actually has a higher level of difficulty.

Bang! contributed by students at Terrell High School, Terrell, TX (1998-1999).

35. The Buzzer Game

Objective: Effectively make "buzzed" lines different from previous delivery
Target areas: Listening, creative thinking, timing, self-control
Performance time: 5 minutes each
Requirements: Buzzer or bell (student may buzz with mouth), performance space
Group size: 2 actors per round

- Two students play, acting out a scene chosen by the audience. At any time during the scene, the teacher (or a student) will buzz the actors, who must then redo the last line differently. Because it can become problematic, scenes are usually limited to five or six buzzes, at which time the actors must wrap it up.
- Use this technique for rehearsals when the students get into a rut. This will add a freshness to their characterizations and to their line delivery.

- Partners are encouraged to help one another out. For example, if a student has a hard time remembering what he just said or did, his partner, in character, may offer reminders.
- Clarify ahead of time if you want the parts that are redone to be restated (the line completely changed) or just said with a different type of delivery.

Modifications: Buzz movement in addition to lines. Have students try to walk differently, throw a prop with more angst, or sit with more caution.

Try *The Buzzer Game* when you find your students are taking no risks with their choices. For example, if they are continually doing what is expected in a scene or failing to try to identify with potential "opposite emotions," this game will help them to explore the subtle subtext and the author's hidden intent.

36. Touch On/Touch Off

Objective: Find motivation for all movement and speech
Target areas: Awareness, timing, creative thinking, self-control
Performance time: 3-5 minutes per round
Requirements: Performance space
Group size: 2-4 players per round

- Decide if you will play *Touch On* or *Touch Off.*
- The class will define the situation, and the actors will then act out the scene.
- All touching must be motivated.
- Players can only talk when two or more are touching, so each must always be aware of what the others are doing.

Modification: In *Touch Off,* players must continue to talk unless they are touching another player. In other words, the touching allows them to stop talking. The scene is over when all players are touching (or not touching) and a justifiable conclusion is reached.

37. World's Worst Things to Say

Objective: Think on your toes; say worst possible thing considering the situation
Target areas: Listening, creative thinking, self-control
Performance time: 1 minute per round

World's worst thing to say during an operation: "Oops!"

Requirements: Performance space
Group size: 4-8 actors for 3-5 rounds

- The players take the stage, standing to the side. Someone offers a "World's Worst" category, such as "worst thing to say at a wedding" or "worst thing to say when pulled over for speeding."
- As actors quickly think of a response, they step toward the audience and say it, then step back in line. After two to three responses or when responses don't seem to be coming, introduce a new "World's Worst."

Note: This is one of those games that could easily become insulting or crude. Instruct students to check themselves before saying something they would not say if the school principal were present. While the objective is to say something totally unexpected, it is not to become lewd or disrespectful.

Sample Categories:
World's worst things to say to a new father or mother
World's worst things to say at a funeral
World's worst things to say at a technological convention
World's worst things to say at a wedding
World's worst things to say at an elderly person's birthday celebration
World's worst things to say to a policeman
World's worst things to say at a security check
World's worst things to say to a blind date
World's worst things to say at a job interview
World's worst things to say to your new in-laws

38. The ABC Game

Objective: Say lines so that each actor's next line begins with the following letter of the alphabet
Target areas: Teamwork, listening, creative thinking
Performance time: 10 minutes per round
Requirements: Performance space
Group size: 2 players per round

- The teacher assigns two players characters, a situation, and a random letter from the alphabet.
- The first line of the scene will start with that letter, and each player's next line must always advance one letter in the alphabet from the previous player's line. Even though the first word of each person's next line must start with a particular letter, he is not limited to one line or even to using that letter for additional sentences in a turn. Sometimes, an actor will get stuck, and it will be up to the other actor to keep talking to either cue his partner (give him hints) or to keep the scene from dying. For example, if his letter is *L*, he might say, "Lost! I can't believe we're lost in your own backyard." The other player's letter is *M* but if he doesn't respond, the *L* player can continue with hints, such as, "Hey, is that your pool? I didn't know you had a pet marlin!" Hopefully, this will help the other player to chime in. "Marlin! I don't have a marlin!"
- The scene must wrap up on exactly the same letter as it started.

Note: You may find that students cannot remember which letter they should use next. This isn't because they do not know their alphabet well, but instead it is the result of trying to follow the scene. You may want to use index cards with the letters of the alphabet written on them so that one student close to the stage can keep the actors on track.

The ABC Game *contributed by Dan Morrow, Wilson Middle School, Plano, TX.*

39. The Question Game

Objective: Complete a scene using only lines formed as questions
Target areas: Focus, listening, creative thinking, strategic thinking
Performance time: Varies
Requirements: Buzzer (optional), performance space
Group size: 2 actors per round with additional substitutes

- The teacher assigns two players and a situation. Other players wait off stage, some on both sides of the performance area.
- The two players must form every line as a question. They may not simply repeat the previous line or use the same question over and over again, and their questions must make sense.
- If the audience or the teacher thinks a player has fallen short of the goal, he will be buzzed out and the actor waiting on his side will replace him. The new player must take up where his counterpart left off.
- Because this game may go on endlessly, you may want to set a timer to five minutes, at which time the scene will end. On rare occasions, students will be able to wrap this up with an actual ending, but it is difficult considering the nature of the game.

The Question Game *contributed by Dan Morrow, Wilson Middle School, Plano, TX.*

40. Killer

Objective: Use observation to solve the mystery of who is the killer
Target areas: Awareness, eye contact, strategic thinking, self-control
Performance time: 20 minutes per round
Requirements: Index or playing cards (optional), large space
Group size: Whole-group activity

- Have students close their eyes, and tap one of them on the shoulder. This person is the killer.
- Students will then open their eyes and circulate around the room. They must stay moving.
- The killer will wink at various students. Once they receive this cue, they must count to ten and then "die" a dramatic death. They will

remain on the floor the rest of the round.
- If a student thinks he knows the killer, he can raise his hand and say, "I'd like to make an accusation." He will not say who the killer is until two other people have raised their hands. At that time, the teacher will count to three, and they will point to the killer.
- If they are right, the killer dies. If they are wrong, they die.

Modifications: For a less "violent" version of the game, play Snow White. In this version, the witch winks her victims into a 100-year sleep. However, since half the fun is in the dramatic "dying," have students faint dramatically into a deep sleep.

You can also play this game in a more controlled way by having students sit in a circle on the floor.

Would you like to play with them? Pass out cards with an *X* on one. The person who gets this one is the killer. This way, the teacher does not know who it is and can play on even grounds with the students.

Killer *contributed by Larry Wisdom of Van High School, Van, Texas.*

41. Copy Cats

Objective: Fine-tune powers of visual observation and imitation
Target areas: Awareness, pantomime, movement, facial expression
Performance time: 5 minutes each
Requirements: Scenery flat or sheet, large space
Group size: Two even groups and one individual

- Divide the class into two even groups and put one student in the middle; he is the cat. You may wish to give this student a prop or a chair, but remember, each team must have the same things as the cat.
- Position the two teams in straight lines on opposite sides of the player in the middle, and have them face away from him.
- The player in the middle will strike a pose, and when he is still, the teacher will cue the first player in each line to turn to look at him; they may observe for fifteen or twenty seconds, at which point the teacher will hide the "cat" (who stays frozen) with the sheet or flat. The first student in each line taps the second on the shoulder, strikes the exact same pose as the student in the middle, and as

122

soon as that student turns to tap the next in line, the first must stand and move out of the line (in other words, he must stop posing).
- After the pose has reached the end of both lines, the teacher reveals the student in the middle so that the teams may compare. Take note of how their observation improves after a few rounds.
- The object of the game is to "pass the pose" all the way to the end of the line before the other team and to keep the general position correct. The team that finishes mimicking the pose first gets one point, and the team that is closest to the original pose gets one point. It is possible for a team to get both points by being both the fastest and the most accurate. The first team to ten points wins. The teacher is the referee.

Modifications: Start with only one team for smaller or less experienced groups, or have the two teams copy two-person poses before you divide them.

Use pictures from magazines rather than a student in the middle.

Make the game more difficult by giving the student in the middle make a small, precise movement during the few seconds they are first observed and having the teams copy both the movement and the ending pose.

42. The Dating Game

Objective: Express characterization in detail so the bachelor or bachelorette can guess characters' identity
Target areas: Listening, character, creative thinking, strategic thinking
Performance time: 10 minutes per round
Requirements: Performance space
Group size: 4 students per round

- Four people play. One is the bachelor (or bachelorette) and the others are the contestants.
- Player 1, the bachelor (or bachelorette), leaves the room while the audience assigns the other three players identities. These should be multifaceted. For help on selecting identities, see list of characters in Appendix A.

- Set up four chairs. One (for Player 1) should be to one side, and the other three (for Players 2, 3, and 4) should be together. Ideally, Player 1 should not be able to see Players 2, 3, and 4, but if you cannot arrange this, it will not affect the outcome of the game.
- Player 1 will ask questions of the others that will allow them to give clues about themselves. In turn, the three contestants will answer the questions in character, interacting with one another and giving as many clues as possible as to their own and the other characters' identities.
- After a couple of rounds of questions, Player 1 may choose a date, but he must clearly (at some point) identify all of the players' unique characters.

Sample Dialog:

Player 1: Contestant number one, if you were a car, what kind of car would you be?

Player 2: [who is playing a nerdy computer geek] I would be something practical like a station wagon or a used electric car. But I need something with a large trunk for keeping all my spare keyboards and cables.

Player 1: Contestant number two, same question.

Player 3: [who is playing an over-zealous football coach] *(Yelling at the top of his lungs)* I'd be a school bus! Got that, Number 42? Got that? That way I can get all the guys to away games! Now, drop and give me twenty!

Player 1: Maybe later. Contestant number three, what is your favorite song?

Player 4: [who is playing the Frog Prince] Ribbit. I'll "Fly" Away. Get it? Ribbit? Fly?

Player 1: Got it. Contestant number three, if I kissed you, would you turn into a handsome prince?

Player 4: Gosh. Ribbit. I hope so. Ribbit. I'm sick of flies. I'd give anything for a big, fat, juicy hamburger! Ribbit.

Player 1: Ooh. The Frog Prince! How exciting!

(This would continue until Player 1 names all players either by name or by identity.)

43. Forgot My Own Name!

Objective: Create characterizations based on what others say about them; try to discover characters' identities
Target areas: Instincts, listening, character
Prep time: 2 minutes
Performance time: 10 minutes per round
Requirements: Pencil, paper, and tape (or blank labels), large space
Group size: Whole-group activity

Inass and Casey ask their peers yes and no questions about the character's name on their foreheads.

- You can play this a number of ways, but consider your group's background before you begin. Use categories that will prove successful rather than overly challenging.
- Have students write one name of someone from a particular category (see recommended categories below) on a label or small piece of paper and fold it. Labels should still have their backing on them.
- Put the papers in a hat and have students draw randomly without looking at theirs. They should then stick the paper to their foreheads (they may need help from peers (who should keep the contents of their labels secret) to make sure they are right side up and facing out.
- The group then mingles, asking people subtle questions about themselves or dropping hints to others without having to be asked. However, each should never let on that he does not know his own identity.
- As details begin to develop, characters should begin to form. If someone thinks he knows his identity, he may use his name in a sentence or introduce himself. If he's correct, the group will let him know and he may exit (in character) as the winner. After the first three to five people exit, let the remainders peek at their labels, and start the game over again with a fresh category.

Recommended Categories:
People in the classroom
Teachers at your school

Famous people
Historical figures (this is a great game for history classes)
Characters from plays
Famous villains
Superheroes
Cartoon characters
Religious figures

44. Garden of Statues

Objective: Use concentration and focus to stay still while the pointer tries to break other players' concentration and focus

Target areas: Confidence, focus, strategic thinking, self-control

Alexia is about to break when Cody mimics her in Garden of Statues.

Performance time: 15-30 minutes per round

Requirements: Large space

Group size: Whole-group activity

• One person is the pointer and all others are statues.
• The statues try to move from one pose to another without getting caught. They cannot speak or make sounds with their mouths (including laughing, coughing, or sneezing). If the pointer catches them moving or making these sounds (he must see them making the sounds, not just hear them), then they are out. Blinking and breathing are the only allowed movements.
• The pointer goes around the garden of statues trying to get them to laugh or smile or otherwise break character. He must also be quick, turning around at random to try to catch them changing poses. He may not touch them, but he may talk, tell jokes, mimic them, or use whatever appropriate strategy he can to get them to move or break character.
• As he sees actors move, he tells them they are out and they step to the side. The last statue remaining is the winner and the pointer for the next round.

Modifications: With younger students, allow them to move their eyes or fight a smile. However, with older or more experienced actors, remind them that any movement at all can ruin a "freeze" in a scene.

Because the players who are out can become impatient, consider starting a second game to keep them busy. After you have about five students out, pick the quietest one to be the pointer in the new game. Tell all the players that one end of the classroom is for the first group and the other end is for the second. Find some way to separate them. From this point on, when a player gets out of the first game, they can come into the second one. You will find that "losing" is no longer reason to misbehave!

Garden of Statues contributed by students of Wilson Middle School, Plano, TX (2003-2004), and members of Plano Children's Theatre.

45. Mafia

Objective: Use listening, observation, and strategic thinking to find and eject members of the mafia before they eject all the townspeople
Target areas: Trust, listening, strategic thinking
Performance time: 30 minutes per round
Requirements: Deck of cards (at least four kings, an ace, and enough other cards to equal number of players), space for a circle
Group size: Whole-group activity

- You will need as many playing cards as you have players. Of these, four will be kings, one will be an ace, and the rest may be anything. Because of the nature of the game, it works best with about fourteen or more players. With fewer than fourteen, you may want to omit one or two kings.
- The teacher should serve as the moderator for the first few rounds. This game has difficult directions, but it is very easily played. Start by explaining the basic roles of the players:
  ~ The moderator talks the players through the game.
  ~ The night watchman (the ace) tries to discover who is in the mafia without arousing their suspicions. He may then try to get them ejected. If you can figure out who he is, you will have a better chance voting off actual mafia members and not townspeople.
  ~ The mafia (the four kings) try to eject townspeople, especially the night watchman, from the group before the townspeople eject the mafia.

~ The townspeople (any card other than an ace or king) try to eject the mafia before being ejected themselves.
- Have all players sit in chairs in a circle. At the start of the game, the moderator passes out the cards. Each person looks at his card, then places it face down under his chair. The moderator instructs the players to close their eyes, and he checks to make sure all comply. This game is not fun for anyone if even one person cheats.
- When all eyes are closed, the moderator tells the mafia to open their eyes. This allows the mafia to see who the other members are, but more importantly, it allows the moderator to know. He then instructs the mafia to close their eyes, pauses a moment, and then tells the night watchman to open his, again to see who it is. At this point, the night watchman begins gathering clues. He may point to one person in the circle. The moderator will shake his head yes or no, depending on whether the person to whom the watchman has pointed is in the mafia or not. He will then instruct the night watchman to close his eyes. After a pause, the moderator tells all players to open their eyes.
- At this point, the moderator will tell the group that the mafia has come to town and no one is safe. They must use listening, observation, and strategic thinking skills to try to discover who members are and get rid of them. He instructs everyone to close their eyes again.
- The next several steps are typical of the remainder of the game. The moderator will instruct the mafia to open their eyes, and they will point to someone to "eject." When they have done this without speaking and have all agreed on one person, they will again be instructed to close their eyes. The moderator will then instruct the night watchman to open his eyes, and again, the watchman may use pointing to question if one person is a member of the mafia. The moderator will respond with a nod or shake of his head and instruct the watchman to close his eyes. Next, all will be told to open their eyes. The moderator will announce the "death" of the player whom the mafia just ejected with a creativity that will help put drama in the game.
- Ejections are your opportunity to make the game funny, dramatic, or mysterious. They can and should vary in creativity. For example, say, "As you know, Lizzy was an avid photographer. Last night, while photographing the wrong end of a shotgun, there was a little accident, and Lizzy and her camera are no longer with us." At that, Lizzy would leave the circle.

- The remaining players begin making accusations based on what they have seen or heard so far. Because identities are still secret, mafia members, night watchman, and townspeople may accuse. Students will use their acting skills to try to get their peers to believe them. One student might say, "I think Olivia is mafia. When Mr. Morrow told them to open their eyes, I thought I heard her charm bracelet jingle." Mr. Morrow, the mediator, would then say, "How many of you think Olivia is mafia?" If more than half the players (still in the circle) raise their hands, Olivia is charged. Mr. Morrow will say, "Olivia, you are charged with being involved in the mafia. You have thirty seconds to defend yourself." At that, Olivia may try to talk herself out of trouble. She might explain that she had an itch and that her bracelet jingled when she scratched it. She may try to focus blame on someone else. After thirty seconds, the jury (all the players) vote. If half or more vote her out, she, like Lizzy, leaves the circle. If less than half vote against a player, he or she is safe.
- Continue the above cycle (mafia chooses a victim, night watchman takes a guess, victim is ejected, players are accused, accused defends himself, players vote) until either all members of the mafia or all others are ejected. If the mafia is ejected before the townspeople, the townspeople win. If the townspeople are booted before the mafia, the mafia wins.
- This is a wonderful game for strategy. Use the end of each game as an opportunity to discuss what students heard, saw, felt, and suspected. How did strategies arise? Why were certain members really ejected?
- Remember, even if the night watchman is ejected, the mediator should still act as though he or she is in the game. Those who have been ejected must never talk or use eye contact to give clues. They should observe the strategies of those who are still playing.

Mafia *contributed by Elizabeth Evans, an eighth grader at Wilson Middle School, Plano, TX (2003-2004).*

46. You Started It!

Objective: Use listening and observation to figure out who is starting the group's newest trend
Target areas: Focus, awareness, listening
Performance time: 5 minutes per round
Requirements: Space for a circle
Group size: Whole-group activity

- The group stands in a circle.
- One person, the observer, leaves the room; while he is out, the teacher selects one person to be the starter. That person can make any kind of sound and/or movement, and the rest of the group mimics him. The starter's objective is to change often but not to get caught. After he has started, the observer returns.
- Standing in the middle of the circle, the observer can only see half the group, but he can hear all of them. He must stay in the circle and use his awareness to try to decipher who is changing the group's movement. He gets three guesses. If he is correct by the third guess, he wins. If he is not, the group wins.
- Allow the starter to be the observer for the next round.

You Started It! *contributed by students of Terrell High School, Terrell, TX (1998-1999).*

47. Styles Tag

Objective: Combine traditional tag with the limitations created by characterization
Target areas: Character, movement, self-control
Performance time: 20 minutes per game
Requirements: Large space
Group size: 10 per round

- Divide the class into groups of about ten. For safety reasons, only this many should participate at a time. One person is "It." He or she will begin a character trait while trying to tag the others at the pace of that trait. For example, a monkey would chase the others quickly, while an old man would chase them more slowly.

- The others must take on this same trait while trying not to get tagged. If you get tagged, you are "It" and must come up with a new character trait.

Modifications: Play this game with your cast, only the characters must be in character the whole time. Who has the advantage? Who has the disadvantage? Who is a good sport, and who takes losing badly? Now play where everyone must mimic a particular character's style and pace. Can your actors learn empathy for other characters from this?

Chapter 6

Improvisation

Spotlight on

Diane Matson
Professional Actress and Musician
Seattle, Washington

A few years ago, I owned a web site dedicated to helping actors learn the finer points of breaking into professional acting here in Dallas. There were a lot of businesses preying on young, eager actors, and I wanted to help them weed out the bad guys. My main focus was in safe networking and in writing and soliciting articles that would make the journey less dangerous and its travelers more educated. In my research, I came across a hilarious poem about scams, and since I was interested in helping actors to avoid them (scams), it caught my attention. I emailed the person who sent it to me, and he emailed the person who had sent it to him. Eventually, I was put in touch with the poem's author, Diane Matson.

We started communicating by email, and it was obvious that this actress was a genuinely good person. I was contacting her hoping to use her poem, but by the time we finished our first round of emails, she had agreed to write the entire article. She was one of these "anything you need" people — "Anything!"

Even after the article landed on the site and was a huge success, Diane and I stayed in touch. She was in Seattle and I was in Dallas — two totally different markets. But, as actors, she and I seemed to face many of the same ups and downs. There were the dry spells, and then there were the days when you had your choice of jobs. It was nice to know that — even that far away — the business was basically the same. Dallas hadn't reinvented the wheel or the acting industry.

When I started writing this book, Diane was the first person I thought of to grace the pages of the "featured teachers and artists" sections. After all, she does it all. So I asked her, and without hesitation came that all-too-familiar reply. "Anything you need."

Diane Matson is a beautiful actress, but it doesn't stop there. She is also a professional musician who plays a number of instruments and a voice artist. This means she is often the voice you hear, but there is no face to go with it.

She has had principal roles in over a dozen television and film titles, and her list of commercials, corporate videos, games, and theatre productions seems endless. She can communicate fluently in sign language, and she can speak several other languages very well; her list of mastered dialects is enormous. On top of that, she uses a teleprompter, can juggle, plays the piano, scuba-dives, is an accomplished mime, and the list goes on. With all these skills and talents, is there room for more? Sure. There is always room for a little fun and games.

"I enjoy *Murder Mystery.* Four people play, but three are out of the room so that they cannot hear. The audience gives the remaining player a murder weapon you would never think of — like a Q-Tip. When the others return, he kills one of them with the murder weapon using as much detail as possible, so that the one being 'killed' can guess what it is. When he thinks he knows, he, in turn, kills the next player. This continues until the fourth player is killed. Afterward, he may guess the weapon. By playing this, they learn to listen and communicate." You can find more information on *Murder Mystery* later in this chapter.

Diane likes improvisation activities because they teach young people to listen and to work with the flow of a scene — and they don't take any preparation. "There are some people, though, who do not work well without prescripted dialog. They become uptight — they need a routine. When they are dealt something 'unexpected,' they can't handle it." The truth is, not only is theatre live — business and life are live. There will always be something unexpected. She warns, "When things go wrong — and they normally do at some point, improvisation gives you practice in smoothly carrying forward so that the audience either doesn't know or doesn't care. Games are good to grow by!"

For more information on Diane Matson, visit her website at www.DianeMatson.com.

Topics for Discussion

• Define "teamwork." What role does teamwork play in the theatre? In improvisation?

• When you are assigned to write a story or create an improvisation, how do you get started? Have you ever tried brainstorming? Discuss brainstorming and how it can benefit improvisational actors. How can an actor use this method in the middle of performing a scene in front of an audience?

• Coming up with an ending can be the most difficult thing an improvisation actor must do. Many agree that starting the scene with an ending already in mind and working your way to it is the best solution. Discuss this and other ideas for coming up with solid, creative endings without the benefit of planning.

• What are some of the rules good improvisational actors follow on stage?

Introduction to Improvisation

In Plano, Texas, a suburb of Dallas, we have a very large pool of talented theatre teachers. The students compete in a number of drama events, such as the University Interscholastic League One-Act Play Competition and numerous speech and acting tournaments. There are a few improvisation competitions, some places just around the corner where students can take classes, and some professional improvisation clubs (such as the popular Improv just up the road), but little is done in the schools. Most teachers use improvisation, but very few use it to its fullest.

I became interested in improvisation when I attended the Texas Educational Theatre Association's annual conference a few years ago. I had taken some students for scholarship auditions, and while they were not busy with the universities, they attended some of the sessions. They excitedly told me about one session in which they competed to see who would be in that evening's student improv exhibition. The judging continued after lunch, so I returned with them. They had a great time, and even though none of them made the cut, we all left feeling like we had just been told the greatest secret in the world. Young people respond really well to spontaneous acting!

Although I knew kids liked improvisation going into this life-changing session, I didn't know many games or activities for it. My own high school teacher used to set up improvisations for us. We had a great time and always begged for more, but it was hard to come up with enough material to keep a roomful of hungry actors satisfied. My college professors, although tremendously talented, did not focus much on it, either. There were some books on the subject, but they were difficult to read. Telling someone how to play a game is not nearly as easy as showing them, right?

So, about seven years ago — before the popular TV show, *Whose Line Is It Anyway?* came to the U.S., I fell in love with improvisation. It was a lonely love affair considering how little information I could find. I started compiling lists of games, instructions, pictures, and anything I could find. I had my students teach me any game they could, and often I would take the old standards like *Red Light, Green Light* and turn them into learning opportunities for actors.

It was only after I started doing research for this book that I discovered the numerous sites on the Internet with easy-to-understand instructions for doing spontaneous acting activities. It was also during this time that I realized how little opportunity there is for young people to express themselves outside of school in this field, especially in my corner of the world.

My two discoveries led me to a third — quite disturbing — realization, and that is that there are some very strange people out there who are lurking, waiting for eager young actors seeking the very information I was out to find. Most of these are harmless, hoping to market things to the children, but they did send up red flags. In the end, I was able to decipher the legitimate improv web sites dedicated to teaching a skill from those less legitimate ones hoping to lure a young customer, or worse yet. This serves as a warning to you and your students: Be wary of sites that become too personal or have links to non-improv sites. Many exist only because they rely on game submissions from you and your students, but seeking personal information from young people or marketing to them using the guise of an "educational site" is absolutely inappropriate.

One of the most disappointing things I did not find was an organized educational improvisation competition — at least not in the United States. North of the United States border, in neighboring Canada, students compete annually in a team improvisation tournament called The Canadian Improv Games. This is an excellent learning opportunity for young Canadian actors. (See Resource section for offical web site.) As for you non-Canadian go-getters, isn't it time we started opening these doors for our young actors?

Review the section on improvisation in chapter 1 before beginning the following activities.

48. Scenes for Dealing with Social Issues

Objective: Explore the popular use of theatre as personal therapy; use dramatic structure, and a full range of creativity; experiment with ways to resolve difficult situations. The focus here is on making good life choices, not creating great theatre.

Target areas: Confidence, teamwork, trust, creative thinking

Performance time: 2-5 minutes each

Requirements: Performance space, cards with common situations students face*

After a night of drinking, these characters lose their ability to make good decisions.

Group size: 3-5 students per group

*Talk to your school counselor before doing this game. Request that he provide you with a list of commonly asked questions, and invite him to class on the days you plan to do this activity. He will be there to talk to the students about their concerns, and because this in his field of expertise, you will be less pressured to chime in where you may or may not be comfortable. Use the *Generic Activity Planning Guide* on page 26 with this scene.

- Create a number of cards (your students can help) depicting situations with which students are faced at some point in their lives. These can be fictional or real, but they should introduce a problem needing a solution.
- With beginning students, allow them a few minutes to prepare for this activity. Let them break into groups of three to five and plan their scenes.

- Assign each group a card with a social issue. Tell students they must create a scene with two endings from the situation on the card. They will perform one ending, and then they will find a creative "reason" to regroup and do the second ending. Again, they will use their creativity to involve the class in a discussion of the two endings and why one works better than the other.
- Because the purpose of this activity is to help students make better choices (not to make students better actors), the focus of the discussion about the endings should be on what makes a better life choice rather than what makes better theatre.
- One option for making this dual-ending scene a success is to use the freeze element and to allow for a narrating character. Of course, this is an area of creativity where you want to allow your students complete poetic license.

Modifications: Use stories from newspapers or the news about teen or adult decision making, or allow students to use real-life situation-stories that have directly involved them at some point in time.

Encourage students to write monologs and duets about these same issues. Can you find a way to write them into a stylistic play and perform them for your school? This may be a wonderful tool for both reaching out into your community for social reasons and for inspiring potential actors to enter your program.

With more advanced students, rather than having them prepare the scenes, have them improvise the situations. Obviously, they will only be able to improvise one ending. Afterward, if you liked the ending (if it was a wise choice), ask them how the scene might have ended differently and what might have caused that to happen. Then have them act out this alternative. Have students discuss why one makes a better ending in real life, but the other might make better theatre.

Suggested Scenes:

A baby sitter's boyfriend wants to come over, but her boss has strictly said no visitors

A young man learns that someone he fears has done something really bad, but he is afraid to tell

A girl suspects her classmate is cutting herself and wearing long sleeves to cover the marks

A young person is told a secret, something that could hurt a lot of people, and then is told that if he or she tells anyone, he or she will be hurt

A young woman overhears her sister on the phone talking about sneaking out later that night to go drinking

A young couple is thinking about becoming physically intimate

A boy asks his friend to stash something illegal in his backpack

A teen is teased relentlessly and is being pushed to his or her limit

A student notices his or her quiet classmate misses several days of school, and upon returning has a number of old bruises

Discussion Questions:

What is the difference between making a good choice and having a good ending to your scene?

What role does dramatic TV, theatre, and film play in the choices teens make?

Can music and video games influence how teens act? Explain.

What role should we play in each others' lives? Should we ignore things that could hurt others? Should we "mind our own business" when we have the ability to intervene?

How can acting out social issue scenes help teens to make wise choices?

49. Key Words

Objective: Listen closely to details of a scene, respond appropriately, and express motivation for entrances and exits; use creativity to work the three key words into the scene supportively

Target areas: Listening, creative thinking, strategic thinking

Performance time: 5 minutes per group

Requirements: Performance space

Group size: 3 actors per group

- The audience or teacher picks a situation and assigns each of the three actors his or her own key word that may or may not relate to the situation.
- The three will then act out a scene, but whenever an actor's key word is said, he must then leave the scene, clearly justifying his exit. When he hears the word again, he must re-enter, again justifying his entrance. Never may a reason be repeated, even on the same character's exit and entrance. For example, if he hears the phone ring for his exit, the entrance must refer to something different like, "Did you know that you can get two pizzas for the price of one on Mondays?"

- The actors may conclude the scene at any time. However, a good rule of thumb is to end after each actor has exited and re-entered at least one time.

Modification: Find key words that in no way relate to the scene. This becomes a greater challenge, and it can also add to the humor of the scene. One way to do this is to fill a hat with random words and have the actors draw for their key word.

Sample Scene: Three guys shopping for a Mother's Day gift
Noah: [key word *apple*] Man, my mom's the hardest to shop for. She's allergic to everything!
Anthony: [key word *tape*] Not mine. One time, I made her a mud pie, and she kept it! It's still in a little zip lock baggie on her nightstand!
Michael: [key word *pie*] Oh, man, I forgot the tape. I'll be right back. [He must exit because Anthony said "pie," Michael's key word.]
Anthony: Oh, hey, I'll come with you. I wanted to get some, too, to fix my mom's broken pie plate. [He must exit because Michael said "tape," his key word.]
Michael: *(Returning from off stage)* Never mind. You go. Get some for me, too. [He must return because, again, Anthony said "pie."]
Noah: Ha! Using tape to fix a pie plate! What a dork. Oh, cool! I could get my mom one of these cool little magnifying glasses. Oh. No, she's allergic to plastic.
Michael: I'll be right back. I'm just going to go check on Anthony. That guy could get lost in his own house! [He must exit because Noah said "pie."]
Noah: Man! Why couldn't I just make my mom a mud pie? Wait a minute? Is she allergic to mud?
Anthony: [Re-entering because his word, "tape," was said.] Hey! Got it! Where's Michael?
Michael: [Re-entering because his word, "pie," was said.] There you are! I've been looking for you for — five seconds!
Anthony: I was buying tape! Whew, all this shopping makes me hungry. I think I want some apple pie! I'll see you guys at the food court. [He must exit because he used his own word, "tape."]
Noah: Wait! I'll come with you. I'm hungry, too. [He must exit because his word, "apple," was used.]
Michael: Ooh! Me too! We can finish shopping later! [He must exit because his word, "pie," was used.]

50. Switch

Objective: Experiment with impromptu changing of characters
Target areas: Focus, listening, character, timing
Performance time: 3 minutes per group
Requirements: Performance space
Group size: 2 actors per group

- The audience picks a scene including a situation and a setting, and the actors begin acting it out.
- At any time, the teacher may call "switch" and the actors will switch places and characters with each other, picking up exactly where their partner left off.
- This can be especially fun if one actor speaks in a language or with a dialect with which the other is unfamiliar.
- Encourage students to put themselves in precarious physical predicaments. When this is accomplished, switching becomes more of a challenge and a learning experience.

Modifications: Try using this in your rehearsals. It is interesting early on in the process while scripts are still on stage, especially when there are multiple characters involved. Do not allow actors to discuss who will be whom, but force them always to switch with different actors. The way one actor plays a role will inspire the others to try new things, take risks, and become less inhibited. Later in the process, once lines are memorized, actors will be forced to "wing it" when it comes to attempting their co-actors' lines. This will force them to become more aware of the play as a whole rather than just focusing on their own lines.

51. Telling Pictures

Objective: Allow a single moment captured in a picture or article to inspire characterization
Target areas: Character, creative thinking, movement, facial expressions
Prep time: Varies*
Performance time: Varies
Requirements: A variety of pictures, clippings, headlines, etc.; large space
Group size: Whole-group activity
*Use the *Generic Activity Planning Guide* on page 26. The planning guide for activity 3 may also help.

• Assign students to bring in pictures from magazines, newspapers, etc., of people — famous or not. You may even use pictures of animals, insects, or inanimate objects. You will want two or three pictures per student, and you can collect them yourself, too. You may want to mount and laminate them, because this is an excellent resource for character studies and other games.
• Start by having each person pick a picture, randomly or not. Give them two minutes to write everything they can about this individual or thing.
• If it is not a person, the student should try to relate to it as if it were. For example, a picture of a washing machine might be a big-mouthed person who always takes others' "dirty laundry" or problems and attempts to make them clean (or interferes). He should pick up on some of the quirks of the nonhuman item, too, and express those. For example, perhaps the load could become unbalanced and cause him to become loud and obnoxious.
• For the first performance, have each student perform a spontaneous monolog about the character in his picture. This will take about a minute or two apiece.
• For the second performance, give two or three students fifteen minutes to create a scene in which their characters interact. As always, this should have a beginning, rising action, climax, and a clear ending. Each of these scenes will take about three to five minutes.
• Lastly, have all the students gather together in an airplane or party or some other place where various people with no real connection

might meet. They may either interact with no real focus on a scene, or you may have them develop a storyline and complete an actual improvisation. This should take about five to ten minutes.

Modifications: Use this same activity to teach the basics of monolog, scene, and play writing. Allow students to work with the first performance, the monolog, until they feel they have written a good piece. Then either alone or in teams of two, have them turn their monologs into duets, keeping all of the action in one time and place. Have them perform these for the class as readers theatre, discuss them, and make improvements. Again, have them work on these same pieces independently or in their teams and then submit them for performance again. Talk about what makes a good scene and what does not work. Now take the most outstanding scene (one per class), and write a play together as a class using that scene as the foundation. Work on your play in small chunks, making copies for the class as each bit is improved upon. Allow your class to break into teams and assign each team a section or an objective. By the end of the semester or year, complete the play and make copies for each student in your class as a souvenir. Perform your play as readers theatre, or if resources allow, produce it for the community. Take the project one step further, and allow students to submit it to a publisher. The learning will never stop!

52. Zap

Objective: Spontaneously create short situational scenes based on movement and posture
Target areas: Creative thinking, pantomime, movement, facial expressions
Performance time: Varies
Requirements: Performance space
Group size: 2 start, all participate

- Students sit in a circle with two actors in the middle.
- The teacher will give the two a scene and they will act it out. At some point, someone from the outer circle will call "zap" and the two in the middle will freeze.
- The one who called "zap" will trade places with one of the actors in the middle and will then start a new scene from exactly the same physical posture. For example, if the two actors in the middle

were "on the ground looking for a lost earring" when they are "zapped," they will freeze in that position. The zapper will replace one of them in *exactly* the position he was in while seeking out the lost earring, however, The zapper must start a new scene having nothing to do with a lost earring. He might — since he is already on the ground — lower his ear to the floor, and in the voice of Tonto say, "They are in Mississippi, Kimosabe. We are in Denver. There is no way they can catch up to us. Can we please rest now? Tonto's feet hurt real bad!"

- If no one calls "zap," then the teacher can call it and send anyone into the circle.
- Encourage the students in the middle to work with a great deal of action and to get themselves into precarious physical situations. This will motivate the students in the outer ring to call "zap."
- If your outer ring is too zealous, you may have to impose a fifteen second rule. Students will have to allow each group fifteen seconds to get their scene's momentum going before they can be zapped.

Modification: Add a third student to the middle, especially when a scene seems to be stuck.

Here's an idea ...
Take note of some of the more successful "plots" students create while improvising. When you need a quiet activity (such as when you have a substitute or while some students are testing), encourage your actors to write scenes using the previously improvised plots as prompts. Because they tend to think of writing as being somewhat of a chore, reward them by allowing them to perform these for the class. Provide and encourage plenty of helpful feedback, make suggestions, and allow time to make improvements.

53. Dubbing

Will, Thao, and Nick attempt to add their own dialog to a movie they have never seen.

Objective: Students must chime in quickly, pace themselves with the movie, and follow the movie's lead; good for students who are reluctant to take direction or who try too hard to stay in control

Target areas: Teamwork, character, creative thinking, timing

Performance time: Varies

Requirements: Old movie, means to show it

Group size: Varies per scene

- The teacher will select a scene from a movie and assign a student to fill in for each character in the scene. This works best if the students do not know the movie.
- As the movie plays without any sound, each student playing a character will "dub" the voices, creating their own dialog for the scene on the video. Be creative. Rather than trying to mimic the actual scene, students should make the dialog up from the clues in the scene. At the same time, their "audio" should flow with the movie's video.
- Once students have finished creating dialog, watch the scene with the sound turned up to see how they did.

Suggested Movies:
  Casablanca
  A Streetcar Named Desire
  To Kill a Mockingbird
  Bonnie and Clyde
  The Godfather
  Giant
  Great Expectations
  Any science fiction movie

54. Party Crashers

Objective: Portray characters fully in a short period of time to enable host to guess their identies
Target areas: Listening, character, creative thinking, strategic thinking
Performance time: 5 minutes per scene
Requirements: Performance space
Group size: 4 per scene

- Four players are selected, and one of them, the party host, leaves the room. He should not be able to hear what happens next.
- The audience assigns the remaining three players odd characters, such as "The Big Bad Wolf with indigestion," "Benjamin Franklin," and a "rocking ballerina." They then move to the side, and the host returns.
- As he prepares (using improvisation) for his party, the doorbell rings. The first guest (Big Bad Wolf with indigestion) enters in character, and the two interact. The guest should be giving improvised clues as to his character (seeking out Little Red Riding Hood, complaining of a stomachache). After a short exchange, the next player rings and enters, and the three interact. The fourth player then enters, and the party is in full swing.
- When the host thinks he has deciphered a character, he must use the character's name (or description) in dialog. For example, "You would think Ben Franklin here would invent something to cure the Big Bad Wolf's stomachache instead of playing with a kite, wouldn't you?" If he is correct, the characters may then find motivation for leaving the party.
- Each character must remain at the party until his character is identified. The final character and the host are responsible for the ending.

Suggested Characterizations:
The Frog Prince
Gilligan
A shadow
An aged superhero
Historical figures or fictional characters
A movie critic
A pharoah's mummy

Modification: Rather than playing *Party Crashers,* play *The Dating Game.* The "bachelor" will be the one guessing the identities of the "bachelorettes," or vise versa. In this version, the one guessing will ask the others questions, and they will answer in the style of the popular dating show, only in character. For example, the bachelor might say, "Bachelorette number three, if you were a flavor of ice cream, which would you be and why?" She might reply, "Rocky Road, because it rocks, but it's still sweet like my dancing." Of course, he couldn't guess just by that answer, but along with other hint-filled answers and a strong characterization, he should know in short order that she is a Rocking Ballerina.

55. Whose Line Is Next?

Objective: Attempt to work random phrases into scenes while maintaining a sensible plot
Target areas: Creative thinking, strategic thinking, dramatic structure
Prep time: 5-10 minutes
Performance time: 5 minutes per round
Requirements: Writing materials, performance space
Group size: 2 actors per round

• Have each student in the class write five to ten lyrics, famous quotes and sayings, expressions, or mottos on small slips of paper, fold them, and put them in a hat.
• Two actors will take the stage. Each will draw three slips and put them in his pocket without looking at them.
• The class will then give them a scene including a situation and a setting. During the improvisation, each player must pull out a slip of paper and use that line in the improvisation until all of the pocketed mystery lines are used.
• The lines will not make any sense, so the actors must find a way to incorporate them into the scene in a humorous, nonsensical way. The best way to do this is to refer to the line as a quote, advice, something you overheard, or something you are reading. For example, one of two characters talking about the Boston Tea Party might say, "The King doth not learn from his mistakes. Why, my beloved mother always toldeth me" (he takes slip of paper from his pocket and opens it, then reads), "'We have ways of making you

talk.'" His fellow Tea Party character might reply, "What dost that havest to do with tea, Good Fellow?" To which the first actor might say, "Absolutely nothing. My mother was never much good with advice. This whole tea party thing was her idea, you know."

Sample Scene: A young man is asking his dad about the birds and the bees.

Nik: So, Pop, I'm almost twenty. Isn't there something you'd like to say to me before my big day?

Richard: Oh, son, you're graduating from high school? I didn't realize ...

Nik: No, Pop. I did that last year. I'm having a birthday. I'm about to be twenty. Isn't there something you would like to say to me?

Richard: Well, son, there is one thing. I should have told you this years ago. I hope it's not too late.

Nik: Don't worry, Pop. I'm sure it'll be fine.

Richard: Nik, when a young man is your age, there is only one thing on his mind. My Daddy used to have a way with words. Why, if he was around today, he'd say to you *(Reaches into pocket for paper and reads),* "Never wear white shoes until after Easter."

Nik: Gramps would say that?

Richard: He was a stickler for fashion rules.

Nik: Well, Pops, I was looking for advice on something else, not fashion.

Richard: Really?

Nik: Really. You know Brenna? We've been dating a long time, and the other day she looked straight into my eyes and said (reaches into pocket for paper and reads), "Hold the pickles, hold the lettuce." I think she may have been dropping me a hint.

Richard: Son, she was hungry. Didn't you buy the girl something to eat?

(The scene would continue until each player had emptied his pocket of the slips of paper and then the actors found a well-formatted ending.)

56. Movie Styles

Objective: Explore a variety of movie styles; incorporate them into a scene of the audience's choosing
Target areas: Creative thinking, strategic thinking, voice, presentation
Performance time: 5 minutes per scene
Requirements: Performance space
Group size: 2 players per scene

- Start by discussing the "styles" of acting or film (such as melodrama, cartoon, action, horror, western, etc.) and what makes each different. Write as many of these as you can list on the board so that students will have easy access to them.
- Two or three students will take the stage. The class will give them a simple scene to improvise, such as a boy trying to break up with a girl at the library. During the course of the scene, cue the students to change styles by calling out a new one. They should pick up exactly where they left off, only with the newly introduced style.
- Actors should not stop to think, back up in the scene, or discuss what to do.

Sample Movie/Acting Styles:
Western
Melodrama
Shakespeare
Kung-Fu
Soap Opera
Talk Show
Horror
Silent
Musical
Foreign Film
Courtroom Drama
Mystery
Love Story
Opera
Pantomime

57. George Is Late Again!

Objective: "George" will create a character based on what he hears his "friends" saying about him
Target areas: Character, creative thinking, facial expressions, following directions
Performance time: 5 minutes per scene
Requirements: Performance space
Group size: 7 actors per scene

- Select several students to play George's friends and one to play George. While George sits on the side of the stage taking mental notes, the players on stage use his "lateness" to talk about him, giving him peculiar characteristics during their dialog.
- For example, one might say that George is probably late because he is seeing a doctor about his chronic hiccups, and another might say that he has never heard anyone hiccup a musical scale. George notes that his character hiccups the musical scale chronically.
- Allow the gossipers to talk about George for about two to three minutes, then have George enter in character. He must interact with his friends, displaying as many of the characteristics as he can.
- Each gossiper must find and clearly improvise his reason to leave until only George and one other player remain. The remaining two must find a clever end to the scene.

58. Old Job, New Job

Objective: Display primary and secondary occupational characteristics simultaneously in a scene
Target areas: Listening, character, creative thinking, movement
Performance time: 5 minutes per scene
Requirements: Performance space
Group size: 2-3 actors per scene

- Player 1 draws a job from the hat. This is his old job, which he keeps a secret. He then draws another — his new job, which he announces to the class.
- The class gives the players a scene that must somehow include Player 1's new job. As they act out the scene, Player 1 must allow traces of his old job to interfere with his new one until the other players can guess his old job. For example, a waiter trying to serve

a meal can't help but check the customers' pulses and fevers. What is his old job? A nurse!

Modifications: Try giving all of the characters old and new jobs. Also, try playing where either the audience or the other two players do not know the new job and allow them to guess.

Suggested Jobs:
  A gardener
  A baker
  A mortician
  A fashion designer
  An actor
  A taxidermist
  A photographer
  A baby sitter
  A trapeze artist
  A member of a SWAT team
  A hairdresser

Sample Scene: A former gardener takes up hair styling
Stylist: Ma'am, you have a seat here, and your lovely sister can sit there and watch as you get your new, spring look.
Sister: We want her to look young. OK? Can you make her look young?
Stylist: Honey, by the time we get done with her, she'll be the envy of all the twenty-somethings in town! We can hang a sign around her neck saying, "Head of the Month!" Now, let's see what we have here. Oh! Dear. Looks like we might need a little fertilizer — Oops! I mean conditioner! Have you ever thought of putting in a sprinkler system?
Customer: What? A sprinkler system? In my hair?
Stylist: Well, honey, it's so dry! Here. Before we start, let's run a rake through it. (Motions raking hair.) And, I wonder if I should use the weedeater or the mower.
Sister: You're going to use a weedeater on my sister's hair? Are you nuts?
Stylist: Excuse me. What do you do for a living?
Sister: I'm an accountant.
Stylist: Do I tell you how to account? No. So please don't tell me how to mow — I mean style.

(This scene would continue until the three actors have satisfactorily wrapped up the ending)

59. The Beauty Experiment

Objective: Experiment using props blindly in a scene; build dramatic structure; deal with the unforeseen
Target areas: Teamwork, trust, listening, facial expressions
Performance time: 5 minutes per scene
Requirements: Props found in a beauty shop (hair items, makeup, a phone); cups of water, gum, and food; table; two chairs; sheet or tablecloth; smocks or towels; performance space
Group size: 4 actors per scene

Warning: Once your students try this activity, they may never want to try any other ones but this one again! It's a ton of messy fun!

- Set up a table with two chairs. You can cover the table with a cloth if you like, and arrange the props on top. Protect the actors' clothing with smocks or towels.
- This is a messy game, so use your discretion about when and where to play. Four players will take the stage, two in the chairs wearing smocks and two kneeling behind them.
- The two in the chairs may not use their hands; instead, their arms are behind them, and the two kneeling players will wrap their arms around from behind to become the sitters' hands.
- The table between the sitters and the audience is covered with the props. The sitters will engage in dialog while the kneelers attempt to follow the sitters' verbal cues with their hands. For example, one sitter may say, "Did you hear the phone ring?" The actor playing his hands must then find the phone and get it to the sitter's ear.
- Have plenty of paper towels on hand for cleaning up spills and misapplied lipstick.

Modifications: Try setting the scene in a mortuary, in a college dorm room, or anywhere makeup might be central to the setting.

Suggested Scenes:
First makeup application lesson
High-pressure final exams
Experimental makeup on an important person
Lesson on how to do an up-do

60. Superheroes

Objective: Spontaneously create humorous characterization based on a superhero name; complete a well-formatted scene
Target areas: Teamwork, character, creative thinking, dramatic structure
Performance time: 5 minutes per round
Requirements: Performance space
Group size: 3 players per round

- While the other two stand to the side, the first player gets his hero name from the audience. It needs to be something silly, such as "Mimicking Monkey Man."
- Once he gets his superhero name, he will need a situation (which can be tied to his name, but does not have to be), such as someone has stolen the world's supply of bananas.
- He will then start the scene, basically talking to himself or the audience — but in his superhero character. Suddenly, superhero number two appears from the wings, and number one must name him spontaneously, at which point number two instantly begins acting according to his new name.
- When number three comes in, number two names him.
- Once all three heroes are in, they will solve the mystery, and each must announce how he will use his special superhero power to aid in the solution. For example, as Laughing Ballet Boy distracts the thief with his interpretive happy dance, Mimicking Money Man will hang by his tail from the rafters and nab the bananas, tossing them to Princess Prancing Pony, who will ride off with them to safety. They may then wrap up the scene and be "off to save the day."

Notes: Names with two or three parts work better; encourage students not to use actual names because that will lead them to mimic the characters they see on TV.

Suggested Characterizations: Follow the rows straight across or try using one word from either two or all of the columns to create your superhero names. Add your own words to the list, too, or go off the top of your head.

#1	#2	#3
Super	Miming	Fellow
Dramatic	Crying	Boy
Spastic	Cheerleader	Girl
Gloomy	Moping	Man
Patriotic	Politician	Woman
Complaining	Aching	Guy
Peachy	Positive	Gal
Leaping	Leprechaun	Lad/Lass

61. The Bus Stop

Objective: Use a single environment and various characterizations to inspire a group of short, connected scenes
Target areas: Character, creative thinking, dramatic structure
Performance time: Varies
Requirements: Performance space
Group size: Whole-group activity

- In this game, two people must be on stage at all times waiting for the bus, but never more than three. Students will enter and exit on their own, and all entrances and exits must be motivated (but they do not have to be verbalized).
- Each actor gives himself a very specific character and interacts with the others. Not all have to be seated, and some may simply choose to pass by. However, each must have a solid characterization, motivation, and some part in the overall scene.
- Dialog is random, but a scene or two will inevitably develop and carry over into new characters' arrivals.
- Rather than fully developed scenes with beginnings, obstacles, climaxes, and well-formed endings, these little scenes are like glimpses into people's lives. Actors do not have to explore an entire dramatic structure.
- Because this scene keeps going, there will never be an ending unless the teacher wishes to assign a student to end it.

• Due to the nature of the activity, this is an excellent game to play with students who are having a hard time understanding motivated movement, entrances, and exits.

Modifications: Try setting your bus stop in different parts of town, at a particular type of convention, or in a different time period.

Suggested Characters:
A little old woman waiting for her granddaughter's bus
A woman walking her child to the bus for the first day of school
Two lovers having a jealous spat
Two people who have not seen each other for years running into one another
A purse thief running from the cops
A cop looking for an escaped purse thief
A retired businessman trying not to get bored

62. Mannequins

Objective: Work as a team to create one character and complete a scene
Target areas: Teamwork, listening, creative thinking, self-control
Performance time: 5 minutes per scene
Requirements: Performance space
Group size: 4 students per scene

Two actors may talk but not move as two others control all their movements.

• Similar to *The Beauty Shop* game, in this activity, each "character" is actually two students. One cannot move at all, but he can talk. The other cannot talk, but is assigned to move the other student.
• The class gives the two "characters" a scene. The movers must help the speakers by moving and positioning their arms, legs, and heads. The only things the speakers can move on their own are their faces and hands.
• The speakers and the movers will cue one another based on what each says or does. For example, if the speaker says, "What's that sound?" his mover should put his actor's hand to his ear as though he is listening. At the same time, if the mover puts the actor's hand on his hip, the actor might respond by saying something like, "Do these jeans make me look fat?"

Notes: This is a wonderful game for getting actors and nonactors to cooperate and develop teamwork. This can also be a great game for introducing each to the other side of theatre. Have your actors be the movers and the tech people be the speakers.

63. Getting Around

Objective: Use a single environment and various characterizations to inspire a series of short, disconnected scenes
Target areas: Confidence, listening, creative thinking, character
Performance time: Varies
Requirements: Four chairs, performance space
Group size: Whole-group activity

- This is very similar to the game *The Bus Stop.*
- Arrange your chairs like the seats in a car: two in front and two in back.
- Your whole class can play this game, so line up all of the players and have three get into the vehicle, leaving the right rear seat empty.
- The driver starts driving the vehicle as though it is a car, and when he comes to a stop, he "picks up" the first player from the line. When this player gets in the car, he has it in his power to change the vehicle to whatever he wants it to be, but it must be done with his character, movement, and supporting lines. The others in the car will soon catch on to the new vehicle, play off it, or use it as a reason to get out.
- The players should engage this new vehicle in some sort of adventure that will include a conflict and a resolution. This should only take thirty seconds to a minute.
- The front passenger has the job of ending each mini-scene. He must find a reason to stop and get out, at which point everyone will shift clockwise, and a new character will get in the right rear position.
- Continue repeating this process until everyone has been in the car, and then try again! It is okay to repeat vehicles, but reward efforts to keep each one unique.

Suggested Vehicles:
Car
Airplane
Dinosaur
Rowboat
Sailboat
Hang glider
Elephant
Stagecoach
Bicycle for four
Space ship
Hot air balloon
Magic carpet
Race car
Broom
Rocket

64. Two-ringed Improvisation (or Square Dance Improvisation)

Objective: Introduce nonthreatening form of improvisation to beginning actors; create a series of fast-paced improvisations for advanced actors
Target areas: Confidence, creative thinking, dramatic structure
Performance time: 1 minute each
Requirements: Large space
Group size: Whole-group activity

- Divide students into two even groups, and have the first group stand in a circle facing out. Now have the second group make a circle around them facing in. They should be in two rings, one inside the other, facing each other.
- Both rings move to their right.
- Have them rotate, and while they're moving call out a situation, place, or even a key word. Without any planning, they must stop and go right into a scene with the person opposite them. For example, as they are rotating say, "Half-price shoe sale." As soon as you say the first words, they must stop, listen to the prompt, and respond.
- Allow them to move around as much as they want. If they get out of order, it is nothing to worry about. Tell them that as soon as you cue them to rotate, they need to get back in their places.

156

- Because this will be loud, allow groups that simply cannot get started to observe groups who are having success.
- If their alignment gets off a bit and two people (one in each ring) are left unpaired on opposite sides, tell them to make due. Have them swing around and act anyway. This is not so much about staying in a particular order as it is about being spontaneous.

Modification: Put the power of authority in the actors' hands and allow them to stop the rings with their suggested scenes.

65. Murder Mystery

Objective: Offer clues to the murder weapon so that it can be passed along a team to the finish line
Target areas: Listening, creative thinking, pantomime, dramatic structure
Performance time: 5 minutes per scene
Requirements: Performance space
Group size: 4 players per scene

Daksha "murders" Casey with a roll of tape in Murder Mystery.

- Four students play. Three leave the room so they cannot hear about the weapon. While they are out, the audience assigns the one remaining player a weapon with which to "kill" the next player. It should be something that would not normally be used to commit a homicide, like a cotton swab.
- Player 2 comes into the room, and Player 1 must set up and commit a murder using the item the class has assigned him. Because he wants his teammate to guess the item, he must talk about it and justify it before he commits the crime. The more details he can give about the weapon without giving it away completely, the better.
- After he has killed Player 2, he summons Player 3. Player 2 — who miraculously survived the killing (or came back to life) now kills Player 3 with the same weapon using the same tactics. However, he must be completely original in his delivery. He may not repeat any of the things his killer said to him. Player 3 summons the final player.
- Player 3 kills Player 4 in the same manner using the same weapon. Again, he must be original in his dialog, but he must give his victim clues.

- As a part of his dramatic death scene, Player 4 reveals what he thinks the weapon is.
- This is a fabulous way to get students tuned in to the other players, forcing them to listen and watch for clues rather than jumping to conclusions or attempting to control the scene.

Modification: Fill a hat with "weapons" written on small pieces of paper and have Player 1 draw. This way, the class does not know the weapon, either.

Sample Dialog:
Player 1: I worked on that project for ten years, and she stole it, just like that! Oh, here she comes.
Player 2: Hi, Wyatt. What are you doing here in this dark, creepy alley?
Player 1: You! You stole my life's work! I've come to kill you with — *(Pulls pantomimed prop from pocket; holds it like a Q-Tip)* this!
Player 2: No! Anything but that!
Player 1: Ho, ho! You deserve a lot worse, you traitor and thief. *(Scratches ear.)*
Player 2: What's wrong with your ear?
Player 1: Itch. Hang on. *(Uses pantomime to swab ears with weapon.)* Better. Now, don't mind the wax. *Now* I am going to kill you! *(Acts out a violent stabbing with make-believe cotton swab.)*
Player 2: Argh! Hey that tickles! Argh. *(Dies. Player 1 exits to get Player 3, and Player 2 gets up to prepare for his turn.)*
Player 3: Hey, Lindsie, you wanted to see me?
Player 2: Um, yes, thanks for coming so quickly.
Player 3: Sure. No problem. What can I do for you?
Player 2: It's about Wyatt's plans. Have you seen them? ...

(This would continue until Players 2, 3, and 4 are dead and the weapon has been guessed.)

Murder Mystery *contributed by Diane Matson, Seattle, WA.*

Chapter 7

Pantomime

Brian Turner
International Banker
Spotlight on and Pantomime Actor
Cheam, England

Pantomime means different things to different people throughout the world. When some think of pantomime, they think of silent, jester-like characters, such as the one played by famous French actor, Marcel Marceau. Others may be reminded of actors mimicking complicated, detailed, realistic-looking actions without the use of props. Others might imagine a performer lip-synching to a song. In England, pantomime is a traditional Christmastime performance with plenty of brightly colored costumes, funny jokes, music, and fancy sets. It is not exactly what one would call "silent."

At the same time, the term "international banker" does not exactly bring to mind apple-red cheeks, big doll-like eyelashes, brightly colored wigs, and men in petticoats. However, actor, husband, father, and international banker Brian Turner feels right at home in his fun, flamboyant costumes. He has acted in three dozen pantomimes and many plays, and he still enthusiastically defends his craft: "My belief is that if you are rehearsing and performing properly, it is very hard and exhausting work. But, because it is so different to what I do as a job, it is very relaxing. I have had occasions when I have had a lot of stress at the office, but the moment I cross the line from the wings onto the stage, my full concentration is on the performance and I forget all my worries from work. It gives me quality time when I can recharge my mental batteries."

Traditionally British pantomime, also known as panto, is based on the Italian commedia dell'arte, a theatre style in which a plot was written with stock characters. This meant the characters were "recycled" throughout many stories rather than unique to each new plot. Because they were introduced repeatedly, the same actors played the same characters many times. From this, pantomime evolved, and songs and dances replaced much of the dialog to appeal to the masses and to make the performance easier to follow.

Modern pantos, such as those in which Mr. Turner acts, follow much the same recipe. "It's a musical play based on a well-known fairy tale or legend, played with pace throughout, with lots of corny jokes, stock scenes, slapstick, dancing, a principal boy (played by a girl), a dame (played by a man), a villain, actors dressed as animals, fairies, ghosts, spectacular effects, audience involvement." Panto acting is larger than life, spectacularly colorful, and both movement and fast tempo are essential.

At the time that he agreed to be interviewed, Mr. Turner was knee-deep in rehearsals for two musicals, auditioning for a third, and conducting workshops with school children, teaching them about pantos. It's obvious he loves the stage, but what drives a husband, father, and full-time businessman to devote so much to the craft? "I just enjoy performing," he states simply. "The youngsters are just swallowed up in awe and wonder at the whole spectacle, while the adults enjoy the corny jokes and audience participation." This would lead one to believe that the payoff is strictly personal satisfaction. However, he proudly adds, "We also donate our proceeds to a children's hospital. Over the years, we have raised in excess of about $700,000 American dollars. I am very lucky to be able to enjoy playing wonderful roles and know that our efforts are in some small way making a child's life a little easier."

Actions really do speak louder than words.

Topics for Discussion

- What is the difference between mime and pantomime?

- If actors will be using props in their performances, why would they want to learn pantomime? What benefits can learning the craft give an actor?

- How is pantomime like sign language? Might a person visiting another country where he does not know the language benefit from using pantomime?

Introduction to Pantomime

Oftentimes when nonactors hear the word pantomime, the image they get in their heads is actually of a mime artist. Pantomime and mime are very closely related, but they are very different, artistically speaking. *Pantomime* is something that all actors do, and most people use it everyday without realizing it. It is acting like you are doing something or using a prop that isn't there. For example, when you need your sister to answer the phone, but she is busy with a friend, you will act like you are holding a phone to your ear. This signals to her that the phone is for her. If you are on a loud subway and need to know the time, you might point to the area on your wrist that a watch would normally be worn. This is a fairly universal signal for "time," but it is also a pantomimed signal for "please tell me the time."

Mime, on the other hand, is an actual art form. It is an exaggerated performance style in which the mime artists act out places, things, and events without the use of props or set pieces. Their crisp and precise movements create the illusion that they are dealing with actual things that aren't really there. During the age of silent movies, comic actors capitalized on this style of acting because they could not support their movements with natural dialog (thus the term *silent film*). Instead, opening a window became a huge comic moment, punctuated with a great deal of tugging and pushing, force and resistance.

Mime is also associated with a particular style of dress that helps the actor to move freely. Usually black "dance pants" or any stretchy overalls, tights, or even leotards are worn. Mimes are also commonly depicted with black and white striped tops, again stretchy to allow for all types of movement. Jazz shoes help the feet to slide easily for the illusion of walking, skating, or sliding. Hats are often worn and may be used to hide a few small props or to collect tips. Many mime artists carry a variety of hats to help establish a number of different characters. Lastly, most mimes wear simple white makeup with a few defining features in black and sometimes red. Because the costumes and makeup are mostly black and white, they create the illusion of a blank slate, forcing the actor to be extremely expressive, but also freeing him to be anyone or encounter anything his creativity allows.

Top Twelve Pantomime Do's and Don'ts

12. Do keep the storyline simple

11. Don't be in a hurry

10. Do start with the end in mind

9. Do express many creative details about each pantomimed object, such as size, weight, smell, texture, temperature, function, and your character's like or dislike of the thing

8. Do remember where things are and refer to them in the exact same place again

7. Don't mouth words or phrases if you can make them clearer by using pantomime

6. Do introduce obstacles

5. Do establish unique and interesting characters

4. Do introduce clever devices, such as slow motion, unusually large (or small) pantomimed props, lassos, ladders, magic, and tricks

3. Do remember that pantomime is magical: You can possess or do anything you want because the audience is programmed to believe what they cannot see

2. Do position yourself so that the audience can see you and your wonderful facial expressions at all times; there is nothing interesting about your back!

1. Every pantomime must have a beginning, a conflict, a climax, and a clever, well-formatted ending

The activities in this section will exercise your students' pantomime (and, in some cases mime) skills. However, keep in mind that not all of the activities will require total silence. Certain games allow some students to talk but require others to pantomime. Some simply have pantomime as a "side" focus. All will benefit young actors. As you explore the various lessons, adapt them to fit your needs.

66. Simple Pantomime

Objective: Introduce young actors to the simplest form of pantomime

Target areas: Confidence, pantomime, dramatic structure, presentation

Performance time: 1-2 minutes per scene

Requirements: Writing materials, performance space

Group size: All perform individually

- Start with one player; this person will pantomime a simple activity such as a household chore. Discuss his performance. What did the audience enjoy about it? What would they change if they were directing the scene? What suggestions might the teacher offer to improve the quality of the pantomime?
- Next, add a challenge by having him do the same activity, but by incorporating a problem or an obstacle. This is a "moment," not a story. For example, if the actor brushed his teeth the first time, now have him think of a way to make that same activity more challenging, such as being unable get the lid off the toothpaste, or discovering the hard way that someone switched his toothpaste with a tube of glue. Again, after each performance, discuss its entertainment value, and maintain a positive, supportive attitude.
- Once students have successfully completed this phase of the pantomime, have each create a two-minute silent scene with this task as the central focus, demonstrating all the elements of a story: beginning, rising action, climax, and a clear ending. This would be a good time to videotape performances and have the class evaluate their peers on paper rather than aloud. Instruct all the class to watch their own performances and evaluate themselves, too.

Modifications: Try the scene without any dialog and then allow students to use dialog. Note how their movements change when they are no longer focused on them as the only means of relaying the message.

Sample Scenes:
Sweeping the floor
Making eggs
Washing the dishes
Opening a childproof bottle
Cleaning the toilet
Painting a mailbox
Raking leaves
Cleaning the pool
Changing a baby's diaper
Putting on a pair of socks

Simple Pantomime Planning Guide

Name: _____ Date: _____

66. Simple Pantomime
• After having experimented with the simplest forms of pantomime, now you will create a two-minute silent scene with a basic task as the central focus.
• Your scene should demonstrate all the elements of a story: beginning, rising action, climax, and a clear ending.
• There should be no talking in your scene.

You will have _____ minutes to plan this activity

Some samples of scenes you may choose to do include:

Sweeping the floor   Putting on a pair of socks
Opening a childproof bottle   Changing a baby's diaper
Cleaning the toilet   Cleaning the pool
Making eggs   Washing the dishes
Painting the mailbox   Raking leaves

Or you may do another scene, but get your teacher's permission first.

List at least six other ideas for simple pantomimes.

_____   _____
_____   _____
_____   _____

What do you think will be the most interesting choice? _____

Brainstorm some ideas for your scene. Every idea should relate back to your topic (above).
_____
_____
_____

Write the events of your simple pantomime briefly, identifying the basic parts of a story.
The beginning: _____
_____
_____

The conflict: _____
_____
_____

The climax: _____
_____
_____

The ending: _____
_____
_____

Give your pantomime a title.

_____

Now write a creative introduction for your pantomime. Write the final version below.

_____

_____

_____

_____

After you've finished writing the introduction consider the following:
• Is the story interesting? If not, make it more interesting before going any further.
• Can you clearly express all of the parts of your scene in pantomime? If not, simplify it.
When you are ready, practice your silent scene until you are comfortable with it.

After the Performance:
1. How do you think you did?

2. What were some of the comments your peers made?

3. What can you do to improve before next time?

67. Forced Pantomime

Objective: Introduce the simplest form of pantomime with the added element of reasoning
Target areas: Pantomime, dramatic structure, presentation
Prep time: 5-10 minutes
Performance time: 3 minutes per group
Requirements: Writing materials, performance space
Group size: 2 actors per group

- A bit different than traditional pantomime, forced pantomime requires that students both find and demonstrate reasons for not being able to speak.
- Start the game with two students, but one is unable to vocalize his message and must resort to pantomime instead.
- The students must pantomime performing a difficult task. Because one of the students is unable to talk, he or she should take the lead, "telling" the other student what to do without using dialog. Remember, this student must "explain" with pantomime why he or she cannot talk.
- Later, challenge both to be silent for the entire game. Reasons may include (but are not limited to) not speaking the language, having a sore throat or laryngitis, having an obstruction in their mouth, and so on.

Sample Scenes:
  Making a giant sub sandwich
  Building a model airplane
  Performing complicated surgery
  Directing air traffic at a busy airport
  Trying to sneak up on the enemy
  Dressing a mannequin

Forced Pantomime Planning Guide

Name 1: _____ Date: _____

Name 2: _____

67. Forced Pantomime
- A bit different than traditional pantomime, forced pantomime requires that you both find and demonstrate reasons for not being able to speak.
- The activity is done in pairs, but one person is unable to vocalize his message and must resort to pantomime instead.
- You and your partner will pantomime performing a difficult task. By the end of the scene, you will have created a fully developed plot, and you will have expressed why one character is unable to talk.

You will have _____ minutes to plan this activity

Some samples of scenes you may choose to do include:

Making a giant sub sandwich   Directing air traffic at a busy airport
Building a model airplane   Trying to sneak up on the enemy
Performing complicated surgery   Dressing a mannequin

Or you may do another scene, but get your teacher's permission first.

List at least six other ideas for forced pantomimes.

_____   _____

_____   _____

_____   _____

What do you think will be the most interesting choice? _____

Brainstorm some ideas for your scene. Every idea should relate back to your topic (above).

_____

_____

_____

Write the events of your forced pantomime briefly, identifying the basic parts of a story.

The beginning: _____

_____

The conflict: _____

_____

The climax: _____

_____

The ending: _____

_____

167

Sample form

Give your pantomime a title.

_____

Now write a creative introduction for your pantomime. Write the final version on the lines below.

_____

_____

_____

_____

After you finish writing the introduction, consider the following questions:
• Is the story interesting? If not, make it more interesting before going any further.
• Can you express the parts of your scene that must be silent in pantomime? If not, simplify them.
When you are ready, practice your forced pantomime until you are comfortable with it.

After the Performance:
1. How do you think you did?

2. What were some of the comments your peers made?

3. What can you do to improve before next time?

Extension Activity: Explore ways for both actors to be silent for the entire game. Reasons may include (but are not limited to) not speaking the language, having a sore throat or laryngitis, having an obstruction in one's mouth, and so on.

68. The Garage Sale

Objective: Discover a more advanced and detailed pantomime in a nonthreatening activity
Target areas: Imagery and recall, creative thinking, pantomime, facial expressions
Prep time: 5-10 minutes
Performance time: 1-2 minutes each
Requirements: Writing materials, performance space
Group size: All students perform individually

- Students "browse" a garage sale, picking up, trying on, and using a variety of different items.
- Instruct students to explore each item thoroughly.
  - ~ How does it sound?
  - ~ Is it empty?
  - ~ Does it have a smell?
  - ~ How does it function?
  - ~ What happens if you ...?
  - ~ "Excuse me, how much is this?"
- After they have explored the items in the sale, they may wrap up their scene any way they choose, but they must have a solid, well-formatted ending.

Modifications: For beginning actors, try writing various garage sale items on index cards and placing them face down for students to "browse."

Also, if students are not thoroughly exploring an item, have them continue to give visual hints until the audience is able to guess the item aloud.

Sample Garage Sale Items:
A feather boa
An old cuckoo clock
Japanese language tapes
Maracas or a tambourine
A box of moldy chocolates
A scary Halloween mask
A time machine
A fancy cane and top hat
A broken umbrella

A half-eaten sandwich
A baby doll that says odd things when her string is pulled
A magic hat
Dentures
A treasure chest full of gold
A mirror
A black hole
Various tools
A mime

69. The Letter

Objective: Explore facial expression and various emotions and characteristics; learn about timing and the value of silence on stage
Target areas: Eye contact/nonverbals, imagery and recall, facial expressions, timing
Prep time: Optional
Performance time: 1 minute each

Casey demonstrates a number of emotions in The Letter.

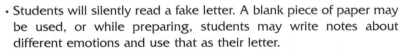

Requirements: Writing materials, prop paper, performance space
Group size: All perform individually

- Students will silently read a fake letter. A blank piece of paper may be used, or while preparing, students may write notes about different emotions and use that as their letter.
- The letter will recount a "story" about various events that would realistically conjure a variety of contrasting emotions. The actors will react to the events in the letter with proper timing and appropriate expressions.
- Gestures, if kept very natural, will aid in the activity.

Modifications: Write several series of emotions on papers and insert them into sealed envelopes. Allow students to pick one envelope each and either prepare the scene (by opening the envelope in advance) or respond to the letter impromptu.

Make the activity an observation game by having students read and react to their letter, then pass it to one person in the audience (as though sharing the letter) and having that person respond to the "same" letter. In this case, the paper should be blank. If the second student has carefully observed the first, he will be able to react as though he is reading the same letter; however, a creative student will not mimic the first, but will instead find reasons to be unique in his responses. Allow him to justify the reactions.

Encourage students to create plots to their performances, including the events recounted in their letters. While students should read the letters silently, allow them to speak before and after the letter is read.

Sample Combinations of Emotions and Characteristics:
Thrilled, nervous, angry
Stubborn, sneaky, friendly
Eager anticipation, shock, disappointment
Anger, joy, fear
Childish, sad, frustrated
Sleepy, cold, frightened
Pride, disgust, love
Pleased, lonely, suspicious
Triumphant, defeated, uncertain
Bored, excited, tense
Perturbed, amused, tired or exhausted

70. The Machine

Objective: Learn the finer points of mime-like movement by creating an imaginary machine; explore timing, teamwork, and precision
Target areas: Teamwork, creative thinking, timing, movement
Performance time: 5 minutes per round
Requirements: Large space
Group size: 8-10 performers per round

Students create a contraption with a number of different mechanisms in The Machine.

- Students will stand in a circle with enough space between them that they can move freely without hitting one another.
- One person will start by acting out a simple machine function with crisp and precise robotic movements. The function may include

171

pulling, pushing, turning, cranking, lifting, setting, sliding, or any simple activity. It should be a repetitive up and down or side to side motion, or it may be a combination of the two, but instruct students to keep it simple.

- After the first person has repeated his function two or three times, establishing a firm rhythm, the person to his left will add to it, creating a new motion. The two motions should be related — a sort of cause and effect.
- Continue adding motions until each person in the circle has become a part of the machine. The last person has the difficult task of either tying his movement to the first person's so that the whole process starts over again or completing the process, thus shutting down the machine.

Modifications:
- Allow students to add sounds to their machine
- Have the students on both sides of the first person add to the machine simultaneously
- Have two students start at different parts of the circle but at the same time
- Give the students a "function" for their machine and have them come up with realistic tasks for each robot in order to complete the function
- Set the robot to music, adding a forced rhythm and theme; how does this alter the students' creativity?

71. Charades

Objective: Add a competitive and fun edge to pantomime
Target areas: Strategic thinking, pantomime, facial expression
Performance time: 1 minute each
Requirements: Writing materials, index cards with names of books and movies on them
Group size: All perform individually

When team members guess a word, this sign for "on the nose" tells them they are correct.

- Divide the class into two teams.
- Provide students with index cards and have them list movies,

plays, books, people, TV shows, famous sayings, and events throughout history, one on each card. Because these can be used again and again, save used charades cards for years. Keep a box dedicated to this game, and occassionally allow students to replenish it with cards listing new films and books.

- A student will randomly select two cards, picking one to act for his team. He will have one minute to get his team to guess the title on the card. He may either act out the event, scenes from the event, the title, or words from the title.
- If his team has not successfully guessed the card after a minute, the other team has one guess to try to steal the point.
- The first team to ten points wins (or the team with the most points after each member of the team has played).
- Allow students to use standard charades strategies:
  - ~ *Sounds like* is a tug on the ear
  - ~ Fingers held up in the air tell how many words are in the title and then which word is being acted out (three fingers followed by two fingers indicate the second word in a three-word title)
  - ~ Fingers tapped on the forearm tell how many syllables are in a word (one finger tapped on the forearm would mean "one syllable")
  - ~ They can pantomime opening a book for a book title, tap their own chest for a person, draw a square with their fingers for a TV show, make quotes with their fingers for a saying, act like they are singing into a microphone for a song, or gesture a movie by acting like they are filming using a camera with a winding motion on the side
  - ~ A finger to the tip of the nose followed by a point to a person means that person is correct

Sample Book and Movie Cards:
Gone with the Wind
Angels in the Outfield
Bridge to Terabithia
My Two Left Feet
Look Back in Anger
Green Eggs and Ham
The Iceman Cometh
Long Day's Journey into Night
Lord of the Rings

Romeo and Juliet
Chicago
Dumb and Dumber
Big Fish
Little Women
It's a Wonderful Life
Mystic River
Jungle Book

72. Musical Pantomime

Objective: Use music to set the mood, pace, rhythm, and to help develop a plot in a fully rehearsed pantomime
Target areas: Pantomime, movement, dressing the stage, dramatic structure
Prep time: 2 hours*
Performance time: 3-5 minutes per group
Requirements: Several instrumental music selections, CD or tape player for each group**, performance space
Group size: 2-3 players per group
*Use the *Generic Activity Planning Guide* on page 26 or the guide for activity 66.
**May also have all groups use the same music and use one CD player to play the piece continually

- Divide the class into groups of two to three students each. The group must balance each person's role in the pantomime so that no one person is sitting out or doing all of the work. Encourage students to select a director.
- Provide each group with music and a way to play it, or tell students in advance to bring their own; headphones are optional.
- Give each group a rehearsal space where they can listen to their song without disrupting others. Keeping the songs a surprise would be ideal, but don't count on that unless you have private rehearsal rooms. If private space is not available, instruct students to try to focus in on their song only, ignoring others' music. Set a limit as to how loud the music may play during rehearsals.
- Students must create a story to go with their music; it should have a beginning, an obstacle, rising action, a climax, and a clear ending.

- Likewise, the characters should be clearly developed, each possessing his or her own personality, traits, quirks, habits, and moods.
- The story should work with the music, starting and stopping with the piece, and following the song's mood and rhythm. If the piece is too long, the students will need to instruct a fellow classmate to fade their music out at a particular spot.
- The performance should include a memorized introduction and a well-rehearsed musical pantomime.

Example: A group gets a Russian-sounding classical piece, so they use their knowledge of Russian history to work up a musical pantomime in which hunger and poverty are the central themes. However, as the song becomes climactic, the old grandmother, on her deathbed, instructs her family to use her small savings to escape to a better place. The scene ends with the family boarding a ship to a new land.

Sample Music Suggestions:
Movie theme songs (careful, students tend to focus on the movie, not the song itself)
Classical and symphonic pieces
TV theme songs
Pieces that revolve around "themes" work best, such as the Wild West, Keystone Cops, the tropics, or romance
Jazz, swing, and big band
Instrumentals
Music from other countries and cultures

Modification: After students have pantomimed the musical scene, have them write and memorize a small bit of dialog to go with their musical pantomime. This will probably need more rehearsal (depending on how much dialog you allow or require), so present scenes again in a day or two for an entirely new grade.

73. Expert Olympics

Objective: Create a scene around a mundane task while taking cues from the announcer
Target areas: Listening, creative thinking, movement, following directions
Performance time: 5 minutes per scene
Requirements: Performance space
Group size: 3 players per scene

- One player is a sportscaster (who speaks), and the other two are experts in an odd sport (such as the dishwashing race or the getting-ready-for-school triathalon — dressing, eating, catching the bus, etc.; they may or may not not speak, depending on the event).
- The sportscaster has control of the scene and can use fast forward, rewind, instant replay, and slow motion; he can call fouls; or he can use any other creative means of enhancing the scene. He can even conduct pre-game interviews with the contestants.
- All three players then act out the sport and each must contribute to the creative conclusion of the scene.

Suggested Events:
Spaghetti eating
Balloon blowing
Moonwalk races
Granny breakdancing
Chalkboard cleaning
Face contortion competition
Tap dancing daddies
Hot dog eating

74. Robot Assembly Line

Objective: Explore teamwork, pacing, rhythm, and movement in the creation of a pantomimed scene
Target areas: Teamwork, creative thinking, timing, movement
Performance time: 10 minutes per round
Requirements: Space for a circle
Group size: 8-12 performers per round

- Have your group stand in a circle with enough room between them to swing their arms without hitting one another.
- The first person starts by performing a robotic task. This should be crisp and rhythmic. This person must remember to create a movement that the next person in line can add to. The movements should each be only a few seconds in length.
- The next person will observe for a moment, and then he will continue the objective, performing a different part of the task started by the original robot. For example, the first actor may start by robotically taking something off a "conveyor belt" and passing it to the second actor. The second actor, after observing the task, will attach a part and pass it to the third. The third may drill a hole before passing it and so on. Eventually it will work its way back to the original actor. He may either continue the process of constructing the item or end it.
- Focus on rhythm. You may even want to use a metronome or set the assembly line to music. Tell students that a play cast must develop a sense of rhythm, and when one works outside the team or breaks the rhythm, the entire cast can be thrown off. Show students how they can have different paces without interfering with the overall rhythm of the cast.

Modifications: Try this silently at first so that all focus is on movement, but then add sound effects. Speed up the assembly after each actor has made his contribution.

Try assigning one robot to malfunction; note how the team handles the malfunction. Have actors "reverse" the assembly of the object.

75. What Are You Doing?

Objective: To focus on objectives and tasks despite mixed signals
Target areas: Creative thinking, movement, following directions
Performance time: 10 minutes
Requirements: Performance space
Group size: 2 players per round

• Two players take the stage and begin doing random but recognizable tasks (they may always start by talking on the phone if they like).
• Player 1 asks Player 2, "What are you doing?" Player 2 responds by saying something totally unrelated to what she is actually doing, and Player 1 must now do it.
• Player 2 then asks, "What are you doing?" Again, Player 1 says something off the wall, and Player 2 must do it.
• Each player continues doing what he has been cued to do until he receives a new cue.
• Encourage students to get their co-actors up and moving, acting silly, and trying new things. Remind them that if they humiliate their peer, their peer will likely humiliate them in return; they should only be willing to push their peer as far as they, themselves, are willing to be pushed.
• Remind students to be creative. Instead of responding that you are cleaning your room, say, "I'm dusting my furniture with two feather dusters attached to my elbows." Instead of saying that you are eating pizza, say, "I'm eating a giant slice of pizza with pepperonis the size of footballs."
• The hardest part of this game is remembering whose turn it is to ask the question. Find a creative way to cue your students.

Modification: You may want to fill a hat with random tasks for students who are slow to say what they are doing or who are hesitant to participate.

76. Mystery Catch

Objective: Explore weight, size, texture, scent, taste, and so on in pantomime
Target areas: Eye contact/nonverbals, imagery and recall, creative thinking, pantomime
Performance time: 10 minutes per round
Requirements: Space for a circle
Group size: Whole-group activity

- One person starts by pantomiming holding something, such as a coin. We know it is a coin, because he "reaches" into his pocket to get it, thinks about spending it, then flips and catches it several times. He then decides to throw it in a fountain for a wish. He makes eye contact with "the fountain," who is really another player, then makes his wish and tosses the coin.
- The player with whom he made eye contact must now catch the coin, and for the first few seconds he has it, it is still a coin, but then it changes into something else. Encourage students to express every detail of the change. The onlookers should be able to watch as the object assumes its new shape — a 200-pound barbell. After his short workout, he passes it to someone, who catches it as a barbell but soon changes it to something else.
- The item will be passed around the circle until everyone has had a chance to catch it and pass it on.
- There is no talking in this pantomime, but noises are acceptable.

Modification: In large groups, there will be some students to whom the others simply will not pass the object. Make it a game and an opportunity to encourage observations and attentiveness by adding one simple rule: Students may not pass the object to a student who has already received it during the round. This will force each student to pay attention to what all the others are doing and to make mental notes as to whom they plan to pass the object after they, themselves, receive it. If a student passes to someone who has already had it in the current round, they will sit out for the rest of the round (or perhaps the next round). It simply serves as a reminder to stay tuned in to the group and to make sure that everyone is treated equally.

Suggestions: Encourage students to explore a wide range of sizes and weights, textures, temperatures, and more. Have them interact with the object, such as sneezing after catching a cat, bouncing a ball after catching it, or crying after catching a freshly sliced onion. Remind them that — in pantomime — anything is possible. Have them toss an elephant, a car, or catch a "speeding bullet" in their teeth.

77. Pantomime Race

Objective: Effectively pantomime a simple work clearly enough that it may be passed down a line of students without changing
Target areas: Imagery and recall, pantomime, movement
Performance time: 10 minutes per round
Requirements: Index cards and marker,, large space, one pen and piece of paper for each team for modified version, large space
Group size: Large, even groups (10 works best)

- Divide your students into two teams. They will stand in two lines facing the teacher. All students in each line will turn their backs to the teacher except the first in each line (the two students closest to the teacher).
- The teacher will write one word (either a verb or a noun) on a card and show it to the student facing her on each team. That student will tap the next student in line on the shoulder. He will turn and watch as the first student attempts to act out the card for him. When the second student thinks he knows the word, he taps the next student in line on the shoulder and acts out the word. This continues without any talking until the last person in line thinks she knows the word. She runs to the teacher, whispers the word in her ear, and if she is correct, she gets the card. Each set of teams plays for five cards. The team with the most cards after five rounds are played wins.
- If neither team correctly guesses a word, neither gets the card. In that case, the teacher may have to hold a tiebreaker. Use the words neither team correctly guessed, rearranged the order of the players, and play until a team guesses the word.
- If the first player in each line is A, the second player is B, and so on, at the end of each card, have A go to the end of the line. For the first card, the order would be A, B, C, D, and E. For the second card, the order would be B, C, D, E, and A. For the third card, the

order would be C, D, E, A, and B. This will allow each player to be the first in line once.

- Because of the simplicity of the words, require the exact word to be guessed. For example, if the word is "book," do not allow "magazine" or "read" to suffice.

Modification: For the sake of allowing the outcome to be more of a surprise, give each group a pen and piece of paper to keep at the end of the line. As the last person in each line thinks they know the answer, they write it down (and go to the head of the line). After five cards, they read their answers to the teacher, who tells them if they are right or wrong. If a tiebreaker is needed, it will need to be a new word (since the teams will now know the correct answers). This modified game can reap some hilarious rewards when the teams say their answers.

Suggestion: Prepare a stack of cards in advance.

78. Silent Scene

Objective: Create a scene in which no (or very little) speaking is used
Target areas: Movement, dramatic structure, presentation
Prep time: 1-2 hours*
Performance time: 3 to 5 minutes per scene
Requirements: Performance space
Group size: 2-3 actors per scene
*Use the *Generic Activity Planning Guide* on page 26 or the planning guide for activity 66.

- Students will create a scene (not necessarily a pantomime, but pantomime is allowed) in which no one talks. The scene must have a beginning, conflict, climax, and a solid, well-formatted ending.
- Because the focus of the activity is on silence rather than pantomiming, discuss the differences with your students in advance. Pantomiming helps actors to express the presence of props when they are not really there. Therefore, the focus of this scene should *not* be on props but on the situation, the moods, the story, and the events.
- To which is this activity more conducive: comedy or drama? Why?

Chapter 8

Nonacting Theatre Games and Activities

C. William "Bill" Klipstine
Live Oak High School
Morgan Hill, California

Spotlight on

Bill Klipstine is the theatre teacher at Live Oak High School in Morgan Hill, California. He uses theatre games extensively in both his classroom and in rehearsals for his shows. "Every game I use has a specific objective," he states. "I never just use them to pass the time. There is always some outcome I have in mind."

Sometimes he uses games to break down barriers of what students see as socially acceptable, like getting two boys to share personal space without either being concerned about what his friends will think. Or he may use games to help a new student or new members of a cast bond with those who have been around for a while. Regardless of the objective, there is one thing Bill Klipstine likes to share with his kids before getting into any game or activity.

"I always start by comparing the activity to the workplace when they are adults." He goes on to explain that, in life, your boss may ask you to do something you don't really feel like doing. Everyone deals with a situation like that at one time or another, just like in class when your teacher gives an assignment and you don't want to do it. "In life," he continues, "those who choose not to do what their bosses ask of them get fired. In class, they fail." He further explains that those who do the job, whether they want to or not, will keep their jobs, and in school, they will pass. "But," he explains, "those who do the job, do it well, and succeed — but they don't stop there — they go on to assist those who are struggling with the job, or they give encouragement to those who are reluctant to participate — they will go on to become the presidents of the companies, the CEOs, the true leaders."

Klipstine feels that many students take theatre because they need to have the credit to graduate; they may or may not want to participate fully. Some take it because they like seeing movies and plays and think they might enjoy acting. These students will work hard and be prepared for class each day. Klipstine also believes that there are those who know that they want to act; they are already aggressively pursuing it as a career or a serious hobby. These are the ones who will take great risks with their acting, and they will never complain about working up a sweat. Many teachers assume that these last students are the artists in their classes, but that's not necessarily true. "All of these students, even the reluctant learners, have the potential to be artists," Klipstine defends. He explains that all kids are striving to be better communicators and that their inner actor is just waiting to be tapped. "They must first feel they have permission to express themselves, and then they must know it is okay to enjoy doing it."

Topics for Discussion

Because this chapter is mainly for the teacher's use, these questions are intended for self-contemplation.

- Why is making learning fun important?

- What are some things you learned earlier in your life that you will never forget because the teacher made it fun for you? Are there some special teachers you are fond of because they made learning fun?

- Why are actors drawn to the stage? Why are techies drawn to the technical side of theatre? What is it that draws people to the things they love? Why are people's interests so different?

making Learning fun

Besides activities to help actors improve their acting skills, there are a number of fun ways to help theatre students learn nonacting skills, too. Obviously not all activities you use in your classroom can be "fun and games," but many can. When your students are enjoying the learning experience, they are willing participants. Having a room full of willing learners beats a captive audience of clock-watchers any day! These activities made me a happier teacher, and I was able to carry that into my home at the end of every day. The rewards for a little extra work and a higher level of creativity are great any way you look at it.

One of my favorite times of each school year is when I get to teach my students about costuming. Having only worked at schools without sewing machines, I was forced to make this a visual unit rather than hands-on. That just wasn't the kind of teacher I strived to be, so out of necessity, I discovered a way to teach students how to create costumes without the required tools. Each group, armed with a picture of a period costume, a roll of tape, several pairs of scissors, and a huge stack of newspapers (butcher paper works, too) would make disposable costumes directly on one of their fellow students and then entertain area classes with a fashion show. Oh! Don't forget your camera. These will become some of your more prized photographs.

Theatre history — we're talking several thousand years of it — can test the limitations of even your most eager actors. I broke it down into smaller chunks, taught each of these separately, referred to them as often as I could throughout the year, quizzed students regularly (but only took grades when I warned them it was coming), and then introduced a life-size board game in which students played the pieces and competed to see who could get to the finish line first. My classroom was in the basement and was always cold, so I kept a microwave and plenty of hot chocolate. The winner got hot cocoa for a week! You can use this same activity to teach any theatre terminology, to prepare for semester exams, to teach about playwrights and their works, and much more.

As you approach each lesson, ask yourself several questions:

- How important is the information I am passing on to my students? How will they use it in their lives whether or not they choose careers in theatre? Am I sharing the information with them because it is important or because I need a lesson?
- If the information is important, how can I ensure that the students will remember it? How can I tie it to their futures so that some day

184

they will recall the information without any effort? Can I make the information or skill like "second nature" to them?
- What vocabulary or new words should I introduce?
- What new skills are involved, and why are these skills valuable to my students?
- How can I make their learning fun?

Remember that not everything you teach students will have some obvious value right then and there. Unfortunately, there is quite a bit, not just in theatre but in all classes, that we teachers must pass on to our students that will help them to learn or understand more important matter later in their educations. For example, knowing theatre history may seem trivial to a ninth grader today. However, when he is a senior studying economics or political science, his knowledge of the Greek playwriting competitions or the decline of the quality of theatre in Roman times will seem more valuable. You must lay the foundation for their future learning today.

In this chapter, you will find "lessons" rather than games for teaching students some of the seemingly mundane tasks necessary for laying their theatre education foundations. Adapt them to fit your needs or to teach those lessons you feel are difficult to make interesting.

You will also find several activities for getting things done at the production level of your program.

79. Getting to Know You Bingo

Objective: Learn about each other's strengths, interests, and experiences
Target areas: Getting to know you
Performance time: Varies
Requirements: Bingo-style card, writing utensils, awards
Group size: Whole-group activity

- If you don't already have a blank Bingo-style card, you need one. You can use it for numerous activities, but this one is the best. A blank card is five spaces across and five down for a total of twenty-five large (about 1") empty squares in a grid. For this game, you do not need a word across the top (as in Bingo), but for some versions, find an appropriate five-letter word like *actor* or *dance*. *Drama* will not work, as you need five different letters, and in drama, the letter *A* repeats.

• Provide students with your 5 X 5 grid. You can fill in the topics ahead of time, or write them on the board and let the class fill them in randomly (it's more of a game this way) as they come in. Try to offer more than twenty-five topics so that every board is slightly different. Instruct students to write the ones into their grid that they believe will match the people in their class. Topics should include as many theatre-related statements as possible, but some that are not. This way you will learn what you can about your class, and not just about your actors.

Getting to Know You Bingo

Find classmates who can honestly say one of the statements is true about them, and have them sign below the statement that fits them. Depending on the size of your class, you may need to have each person sign your card more than once. The first person with a full line (across or down) wins. Then see who can get an X first (corner to corner), a frame (all the outer spaces), and a blackout (all the spaces). Have fun learning about your classmates!

I like to act.	I don't like to act.	I like to sing.	I like to dance.	I like to write.
I like to make people laugh.	I like to take pictures.	I like to be in charge.	I prefer quiet activities.	I prefer being active.
I like working with technology.	I am more artistic than technological.	I like to build things.	I have been in a play.	I have been to see a play.
I like to read quietly.	I like to read aloud.	I enjoy public speaking.	I am organized.	I am creative.
I am strong.	I like math.	I like science.	I like language arts.	I like gym class.

- Instruct students to write the topic as small as they can to leave room for a signature in the square. You have twenty-five squares. If you have twenty-five or more students, allow one signature per person, per card. If you have fewer students, allow each to sign fellow students' cards two to three times, or how many times will be needed to fill in the entire card.
- After students have filled in their grids with the topics, the game begins. As in the original Bingo game, they will attempt to get a full line of signatures. After you have had a winner in the straight line category, request an X (from corner to corner going both ways). After that, you can request a frame (all the outer squares) and then a blackout (every square on the board). Award winners with pieces of candy, stickers, or pencils.
- This is a terrific way to get your new students to learn about their peers. You can play this game with vocabulary, too, by saying the definition and having students seek the term on their boards. Put playwrights' names in the squares and have students match them to their works. Of course, with these last two suggestions, students stay in their seats and work independently.

80. Not Just Another Board Game

Objective: Teach vocabulary, theatre history, or other information-intensive subject
Target areas: Learning information, following directions
Performance time: Varies
Requirements: Giant board game, index cards and markers, large dice (optional), large space
Group size: Whole-group activity

When teaching new vocabulary or especially the numerous facts in theatre history, try this activity.
- Use tape or string to make a giant board game on your classroom floor like the simple grid used in *Chutes and Ladders* or the circular "team" board in *Trouble*.
- Have students create fact cards using index cards and brightly colored markers. You can even make a giant pair of dice out of a large, square box.
- Now all you need are the game pieces. That's easy! The students will be their own game pieces, standing directly on the life-sized, customized board.

187

• Create your own rules and play the game. Students will have fun learning their facts and seeing who can be the first to the end.

Suggestions: Set out a basic and simple board using colored paper plates or large squares of paper. Each plate or square equals one space. Customize your game by having colored spaces coordinate with card categories or specific challenges.

The simplest way to play is individually, but you can also play in teams. Start by rolling the dice. Don't move yet. First you must draw a card and correctly answer the question. If you get the answer right, you may move that number of spaces. The first person to make it to the end wins (if playing in teams, all members must make it to the end).

Your life-sized game will be more fun if there are improvisation challenges along the way. Allow players to avoid a trap, double their roll, or send another player back five spaces if they can successfully meet a challenge. Some suggested challenges include making someone from the other team laugh in less than fifteen seconds or getting the player's own team to guess a charades-style card in under thirty seconds. Can you think of some others? How about bonus moves for players who can do a trick like wiggle their ears or mimic a famous cartoon voice? Be creative. There are innumerable ways to have fun and learn at the same time.

Use this game to teach:
Theatre history
Acting terminology
Technical theatre terminology or safety
Playwrights and their works
Current theatre events

81. Stage Maps

Objective: Learn stage directions and blocking terminology
Target areas: Learning information, confidence, following directions
Performance time: Varies
Requirements: Index cards with stage directions written on them and photocopies of each, stage
Group size: All perform individually

With younger students, grasping stage directions and blocking terminology can be difficult. It's hard enough to remember one's own left and right. In theatre, you must remember stage left and stage right — and then you have to figure out whose left and right the director means. Here is a fun and simple way to help your young actors to master the concept and to get used to being on stage.

- Create a series of index cards with various stage directions written on them. These should include a series of directions with multiple crosses and actions. Number them and then make a copy of each on your school's copy machine.
- Take your students to the stage and have them each draw a card. As they take the stage, they will give you their card number so that you may find the matching one on your copy. To start, simply have each student walk through his directions while you check for accuracy.
- Afterward, have them mix their cards up again, leaving them in a pile center stage. Divide the group into two even teams. As in the game *Red Rover*, a team will call on a player from the other side to select a card randomly and walk through its directions. If he is accurate, he stays with his team. If he is incorrect, he goes to the other team.
- The goal is to get all the players on your team. However, as this is a fairly easy skill to master, you will find that players soon do. At this point, reward them for their learning by allowing them to play *Red Rover* the old fashioned way. Be careful! The *Stage Maps* way is much safer!

82. Prop Scavenger Hunt

Objective: Gather props for performers
Time: 2-3 hours
Requirements: List of needed items, several one-gallon plastic resealable bags per group, prizes and/or incentives
Group size: Groups of 5-6 students, drama club members, parents, and volunteers

There are so many things that we need in theatre that other people have. Shoved in the backs of their closets, hidden away in their attics, or boxed away in their basements, average people possess valuable treasures — that is, if you are a theatre teacher. To their present owners, they are junk, but to you, those old Halloween costumes and wigs are priceless treasures just waiting to be transformed into usable stock pieces.

Whether for your stock or for a particular show, host a scavenger hunt for items just like these — treasure to you, junk to someone else.

- Divide your group (cast, drama club, volunteers) into teams of four to five people each. For safety reasons, make sure you have at least one adult assigned to each team.
- Provide each team with a list of the items you seek and a handful of one-gallon plastic resealable bags. Each item on the list should be assigned a point value. For example, if you need sewing notions more than feather boas, make notions worth five points and boas worth one.
- Small items like notions can be counted by designating a volume ahead of time. That's what the resealable bags are for. Tell the groups that they will get partial points for partially filled bags and full points for bags that are filled to their limits.
- Instruct teams to gather as many items as they can for as many points as possible. Remind them to start at their own homes, never go into strangers' homes, and to represent your organization well.
- Have the groups meet back again two to three hours later with their items. The group with the most points wins! You can solicit prizes from local restaurants and stores. Use family packs of tickets to your shows as incentives, and if you have any old fundraiser items or show shirts, throw those in, too.
- Don't forget to announce your scavenger hunt results (with pictures, of course) in the local paper. Include a list of all the items you still need, and no doubt you will get them thanks to the article.

83. Ticket Pre-sales Contest

Objective: Sell tickets before a performance
Time: Two weeks before show opens
Requirements: Tickets, prizes for winners

When doing a show, whether it be a traditional play or a night of improvs, there are many reasons to sell tickets in advance (prior to the night or nights of your show). Despite the many benefits, there are quite a few schools who do not, or perhaps can not, take advantage of this great device.

First, selling tickets in advance is a fantastic way to raise money for your show before you open. For example, if you are a new program without a budget or perhaps you have simply misjudged your expenses and are running a little short, this could be your solution. Selling tickets in advance will give you the money you need to open your show without having to cut too many corners.

Second, it builds your audience. There are always going to be those well-wishers who say that they will come to your show, but they are still just thinking about it. They do not mean to be wishy-washy. They just haven't had a reason to make the commitment — yet. For every well-meaning no-show you encounter, your student actors are experiencing the same thing. Nip this problem in the bud by having a reduced price for tickets purchased before your opening. For example, if your tickets are usually five dollars, make that your advanced price, and make tickets bought at the door six dollars. The truth is, you won't lose an audience member over a dollar — they will still come if they do not buy their tickets ahead of time. However, everyone loves a bargain, and if they know they will save money by getting theirs early, even the wishy-washy will commit. Once they have paid five dollars for a ticket, they will come to the show (and if they don't, you still made five dollars!).

Lastly, having students and their parents sell tickets will alleviate two kinds of stress: yours and the box office's. First, you will have to do a lot less marketing, because the students will be doing much of it themselves. After all, it is their show, right? By having a competent parent in charge of the event, you are allowed to focus on your play at a time when it needs it most. As for the box office, selling tickets ahead of time will allow patrons who already have theirs to proceed straight to the usher. You will eliminate those long lines at the box office, and if you have concessions, those who just want to wait in line can join that one! Either way, you have more audience members, more revenue, and less stress.

Students in your show will appreciate the availability of tickets ahead of time, but their parents will be truly thankful. Don't forget to solicit the help of students who are active in your program but who are not in your show. They will enjoy being involved and being in the running for the prizes.

- Find a parent or two to run this for you.
- Start by having these parents seek donations for prizes, or again, you may use old show shirts, fundraiser items, ads in the program (you will need to end your contest with enough time to insert the ad), or family packs of tickets as prizes. Have a first, second, and third prize. That way, if one person shoots to the lead early in the contest, the others do not think their efforts are hopeless. You might even have a patch or trophy for anyone who sells a minimum number (your proceeds will more than cover the cost).
- Be sure your tickets are numbered or have students write their names on the backs as they are checked out to them. This will prevent theft, and if they are lost or misplaced, you can have ushers keep an eye out for the missing tickets (just in case they are found by someone who would sell or use them).
- Start about two weeks before your opening. Each student will check out the same number of tickets. Ten is a good number, because it will make taking their money easy ($5 X 10 = $50, $6 X 10 = $60). Do not allow them to check out more tickets until they have turned in money from the previous lot. However, do allow groups who request more than that number to take more. There are times when a family alone will buy twelve or fourteen, and they will request several more for their friends.
- Consider not taking cash for the contest. This way, if students lose the money, it can be traced. Instruct parents to replace cash quickly with a check.
- Gather money at least twice a week, but daily is best. Post the results so that students can see who is in the lead.
- On the final day of the pre-sales contest, take up all money and tickets. This may even be your opening night, so it is more important now than ever to have a parent managing tickets and money so you can focus on your show.
- Now tally the results and announce your winner!

84. Poster Design Contest

Objective: Obtain a design for a promotional poster for a performance
Time: Enough time before the performance for artists to submit designs and you to judge and print them
Requirements: List of poster requirements and preferences; prizes for winners

Another fun way to involve your students — or perhaps a different group of students — in your theatre program is to host a poster design contest. Many theatre arts programs have their students do the art for the posters, but by making it a contest, you have again created a challenging environment for your young learners. Face it, kids are competitive, especially actors. To ignore this aspect of their beings would be to turn our backs on one of their learning styles. On the other hand, you can use it to pull from them something many of them would never otherwise attempt. You can allow them to feel important and involved.

- Ask your art teacher to head the efforts.
- Again, seek prizes or set aside a small cash prize for the winner (see your campus office manager for your district's policy on cash prizes). Consider having a first runner-up. Their art could be the cover for your program. Additional winners, if you chose to have them, could be showcased inside the program.
- Check printing prices in advance. If you cannot afford a full-color poster, request all submissions be made on white paper in black ink.
- Announce your contest. Be very specific in your design preferences. For example, if you are doing Celeste Raspanti's *I Never Saw Another Butterfly*, explain to students what the show is about. Based on the title alone, you may get a number of happy butterfly posters. However, telling your potential designers that the play is actually about the Holocaust will help them to create something more suitable. If you have a color scheme and are doing color posters, you may wish to include that information in the contest rules.
- Remember to request a design that will either include all of the pertinent play information or leave enough room to include it.
- At the deadline, have your art teacher narrow down the selections, or you may wish to do that yourself. Announce your winners in the

local paper, and remember to provide them with copies of the poster art, too. You will probably need permission from the artists' parents' to use their names both in the news release and in your printing.

• On the nights of your show, have your art teacher create a gallery of all the submissions or maybe just of the top few.

• Scan the winner's art and return the original to him. It is generally considered a nice gesture to place the winner's art in a matted frame with their name and the contest outcome on a small brass plaque.

• Request your local frame shop to frame the scanned and printed copies for you. By displaying these proudly in your office or classroom, you are letting future artists know that their efforts will become a legacy.

85. Newspaper Costumes

Objective: Introduce and increase appreciation for the process of costume-making
Target areas: Creative thinking, strategic thinking, teamwork
Time: 2-3 class periods
Requirements: Pair of scissors, newspaper, plastic bag, and roll of masking tape per group; photos of costumes; cubes or step units (optional); camera
Group size: 5 students per group

Students explore the basics of costuming by making disposable costumes.

Okay, this really isn't a game, but it's so much fun, it just had to be included in this book!

Do you have a sewing machine in your classroom? Even if you do, do you really have time to teach students about making costumes? Probably not. Here is a fun and very basic way that all of your students — yes, even boys — can have fun discovering costumes. No, they will not know how to sew afterwards. The truth is, they will not know much more about costumes after they do the activity than before. The benefit is in the discovery.

By intently observing a picture, your students will discover how a costume is put together, how the lines intersect, and how it fits and even manipulates the body. They will appreciate how much is involved in the construction of a single costume, especially when, at the end of their project, their hard work is torn from the model and tossed in the trash. Remind them that when you sew a costume, it is worn only a short while before being stored away in a closet.

No, this activity will not create a classful of costumers, but it will create a classful of costume appreciaters.

- Instruct each student to bring scissors, a daily newspaper, a plastic bag, and a roll of masking tape. They may also opt to bring cameras (and don't you forget yours!).
- In advance, print, cut out, copy, or provide photos of costumes you want the students to make. The rule of thumb is the bigger the better. Tom Tierney's paper doll books make beautiful examples, with costumes from every era, every continent, and every walk of life.
- On the first day of the activity, break students into groups of about five. Give each group several pictures from which to select their costume. It is best to provide several male and several female costumes for each group.
- Have them select a model from their group.
- On the first day, they should begin making ruffles, pleats, and adornments for their costumes. These are smaller or more difficult items that will take up most of their time. By tackling them ahead of time, they will exercise more patience and even the model may participate.
- You will want to show them how to do some of the less obvious tasks, such as making folds and tucks and gathering the tops of "skirts" so that they "pouf" out. At the end of the period, carefully store these pre-constructed items away in the groups' plastic bags until the next class period.
- Remind models to wear clothing that will allow their group to construct the costume directly onto their bodies. Tank tops, leotards, dance pants, or tights would be best, but body-hugging sweat pants and a T-shirt will work, too.
- On the second day, the groups should get right to work putting their costumes onto their models. They will cut and tape the newspaper into the shapes that costumers would cut and sew fabric.

- Place models onto a cube or step unit so that their group may easily work without crouching. This will also allow trains and long skirts to flow and drape without getting too crinkled.
- When the newspaper costumes are complete, take plenty of pictures of the models and their hard-working groups. If you have a class near you who is willing, invite them to come see the finished products or take your models out for a fashion show.
- These pictures make a great bulletin board!

86. Character Collage

Objective: Develop character; become more sensitive to character's deeper levels and relationship to others; draw parallels between character and other parts of play
Target areas: Character, creative thinking
Time: Several class periods
Requirements: Materials to construct collages

Okay, so this activity isn't a game either. Still, it is so much fun and so useful, it just had to be in this book.

Use character collages early in your rehearsal process if you are doing a show or early in your scene work when studying monologs and duets in class. Students will become more sensitive to their characters' deeper levels, and they will also start thinking about their relationships to other actors' characters. One of the greatest benefits of the activity is that they begin exploring the symbolism of the literature without realizing that they are doing so. At the same time, they are drawing parallels between their character, the title of the play, dialog and subtext, and what others in the class or cast think of their character.

There are several ways to approach this activity. The first is to create character masks. Your students will love this method because they will have a piece of art that they can appreciate when the lesson is over. It is also a great Halloween-time lesson. If you choose to do this collage, remind students that these are not masks to be worn. Instead, they are decorative symbols of their characters. When they are finished, they can be hung from curling ribbon or fishing line from your ceiling (if they are two- sided) or your wall (if they are one-sided).

You can also make script covers or notebook inserts. This is more functional and will probably have more of an impact on your actors. If they are seeing the completed collages on a daily basis, the words and images they chose to symbolize their characters will become more deeply ingrained in their own acting.

Finally, have students create simple copy-paper sized collages. These are the fastest way to use this kind of imagery to explore the symbolism of characters, and they, too, can be displayed on your classroom wall.

Character Collage Masks

- Instruct students to bring a one-gallon resealable bag, several old magazines, scissors, and glue to class. They may also want to bring feathers, beads, sequins, glitter, or whatever they feel would best help to represent their characters. It would be helpful to bring a sheet of thin cardboard (like a cereal box) so that the finished mask can be made more sturdy.
- Have students write their character's name in large black letters on their resealable bag. Tape or place them where everyone can see the names and everyone has access to them.
- On the first day, have students peruse their magazines and find words, pictures, textures, phrases, quotes, or patches of color to represent any character from the play (or from the various scenes). These do not have to be for their own character. As they find things, they will place them in the bag for the character they represent.
- Sit in a circle and discuss the contents of each bag. Depending on your time frame, you may want to spend just a few minutes doing this or an entire class period. If you have a small group, this may also be done casually as your group sits in a circle, cuts from the magazines, and discusses their findings at the same time.
- After the contents of the bags have been discussed, it is time for each actor to choose what to put onto his mask and to complete the project.
- Provide each with a line drawing of a simple Mardi Gras-style mask. They do not have to use this exact shape. Rather, it will serve as the foundation for the shape they choose to represent their particular character.
- Students should glue the mask line drawing to the cardboard before deciding on the final shape. Using a pencil, they should make a light outline of the shape they want their mask to be and then cut it out.
- Have them experiment with the placement of the magazine

197

clippings before gluing them. Also, they should decide if the eyeholes should remain solid or should be cut out.

- If you plan to hang the masks from the ceiling, they should decorate both the front and back.

- After all the magazine clippings are done, they may begin embellishing the masks with other three-dimensional decorations, such as sequins, glitter, or seashells. Provide them with string and a single-hole punch, and they can prepare the mask for hanging.

- When finished, students may turn the completed masks in to you enclosed in their resealable bags.

Character Collage Script Covers/Notebook Inserts

- Instruct students to bring a one-gallon resealable bag, several old magazines, scissors, and glue to class. They should not use any glitter or three-dimensional embellishments because these will get in the way at rehearsal or make it difficult to slide inside the notebook cover.

- Have students write their character's name in large black letters on their resealable bag. Tape or place them where everyone can see the names and everyone has access to them.

- On the first day, have students peruse their magazines and find words, pictures, textures, phrases, quotes, or patches of color to represent any character from the play (or from the various scenes). These do not have to be for their own character. As they find things, they will then place them in the bag for the character they represent.

- Sit in a circle and discuss the contents of each bag. Depending on your time frame, you may want to spend just a few minutes doing this or an entire class period. If you have a small group, this may also be done casually as your group sits in a circle, cuts from the magazines, and discusses their findings at the same time.

- After the contents of the bags have been discussed, it is time for each actor to choose what to put onto their collage and to complete the project.

- Decide whether you will be making script covers or notebook inserts.

    ~ If you are making script covers, take a large piece of sturdy paper (cover stock) and fold and cut it to fit your scripts. Scripts may be covered in the same manner as textbooks. It is helpful to tape the insides of the homemade cover to the actual cover of the script. Once the homemade cover is on the script, students can begin carefully gluing the magazine clippings onto it. For best results, glue clippings onto a closed script and only on the outside of the cover.

~ Notebook inserts are for the large binders covered with a clear plastic pouch. Generally, you can slide a cover sheet into both the front and the back, but for this activity, you will only use the front pouch. Glue magazine clippings onto a regular sheet of copy paper positioned vertically (tall, not wide). This way, the collage will read the right direction when slipped into the notebook pouch.

Character Collage Posters

• Instruct students to bring a one-gallon resealable bag, several old magazines, scissors, and glue to class. Students may also want to bring textured materials, such as sandpaper, cotton, lace, dried leaves, or puzzle pieces — whatever they feel would best help to represent their characters but will not be too heavy for the poster.

• Have students write their characters' names in large black letters on their resealable bag. Tape or place them where everyone can see the names and everyone has access to them.

• On the first day, have students peruse their magazines and find words, pictures, textures, phrases, quotes, or patches of color to represent any character from the play (or from the various scenes). These do not have to be for their own character. As they find things, they will then place them in the bag for the character they represent.

• Sit in a circle and discuss the contents of each bag. Depending on your time frame, you may want to spend just a few minutes doing this or an entire class period. If you have a small group, this may also be done casually as your group sits in a circle, cuts from the magazines, and discusses their findings simultaneously.

• After the contents of the bags have been discussed, it is time for each actor to choose what to put onto his poster and to complete the project.

• Provide each student with a piece of card stock or sheet of chip board. Copy paper will work, too, but it will not be as durable.

• Have them experiment with the placement of the magazine clippings before gluing them.

• After all the magazine clippings are on, they may begin embellishing the posters with other three-dimensional or textured items.

Chapter 9

Developing Your Program

Carla Ford-Rich
Plano West Senior High
Plano, Texas

Spotlight on

For many teachers, especially those in theatre, the "Teacher of the Year" honor seems as elusive as, oh, say larger budgets and a parking space near the entrance. Not so for Carla Ford-Rich — if she had a nickel for every time she was named "Teacher of the Year," well, she would have nearly a quarter! Let's see, there was Vines High School, Shepton High School, and Plano West Senior High. She was a finalist for the district secondary award, and what was that other one? Oh, yes, Texas Educational Theatre Association Secondary Theatre Teacher of the Year, 2004. That's an honor the size of — Texas!

Not only is she a great educator, she is a great businesswoman, too. You have to be to run one of the state's most successful theatre programs. She will be the first to tell you that the program's success is not about size, it is about quality and about meeting your students' needs. "If you have a large number of students who are planning on majoring in theatre, then you must spend time preparing them for that endeavor. Spend time on the audition process, acting philosophies, and techniques. On the other hand, if you have a lot of kids who are interested in theatre but have no desire to pursue it as a career, spend more time on literature and analysis. Teach them to appreciate productions from an audience's perspective." She adds, "The program needs to be well-rounded, but ultimately it needs to be something that the kids find relevant."

While most teachers can admire that philosophy, administrators see success differently — in terms of numbers. Many theatre teachers struggle with getting the required enrollees principals must have to justify keeping a program pure (theatre only, no speech, etc.). How does Mrs. Ford-Rich ensure that her numbers stay strong? "I use a lot of public relations. I have done shows for the schools that feed into our program, and we also advertise heavily across our district and within the community. We work with the feeder middle and high schools when they need it, too, and we always try to see their shows and write letters to the individual actors when we can. Sometimes on our campus, different organizations will ask for help with skits, and we always try to give them what they need. We also support the other organizations like athletics, choir, and band by attending their events. It's all about forming good, strong relationships."

She advises teachers struggling with growth to start by creating fun in the classroom but to always connect games with their target objectives. "I feel a number of teachers use 'games' as a baby-sitting tool more than an acting activity. The student needs to see the relevance. As a matter of fact, I never even use the word 'game' when talking about an acting activity." She also recommends forming strong bonds with other schools in a cluster (aligning campuses). "Perhaps you can even do a show with them," she suggests.

Mrs. Ford-Rich credits some of her program's growth to an improv troupe she formed a few years back. Her high school actors would explore serious teenage issues through role playing. "We did these improvisations for elementary groups and that would open up a discussion for the leaders and students. My actors were given topics in advance, and we worked them out prior to visiting the other campus."

The benefits of performing these scenes for children obviously include guiding youngsters toward healthier personal choices, but there was another payoff that took a few years to realize. Because their audiences were so young, the theatre arts enrollment did not increase immediately, but many of those students remembered the impact their teen visitors had on them, and they eventually migrated toward the senior high program. Just recently, PWSH started a new improv troupe. "I am seeing a lot of new students. They aren't in my theatre classes yet, but one can hope!"

Topics for Discussion

Because this chapter is mainly for the teacher's use, these questions are intended for self-contemplation. However, sharing them with your drama club may be beneficial.

• Are you happy with your program at its present state? Do you want to see it develop further? Where do you hope to see it by the end of this school year? In two years? In five? In ten?

• Just as individuals can benefit from goal-setting, you can develop your program the same way. What are some ways you can make yours better? Have you visited some of the schools in your area who are setting the bar higher? Have you written your goals and established a plan for achieving them?

• People who think positively achieve more than those who are considered negative thinkers. Why is this? Are you are positive or negative thinker? How can what you think affect what you say, and vise versa? How can this, in turn, affect how you grow as a person?

Now that your students have learned all about games, improvisation, exercises, mime, and pantomime, put all this new-found knowledge to work for you. There are a number of ways to use these fun, spontaneous activities both to make money for your theatre program and to build it into a stronger, larger, more notable organization.

Theatre Classes

The strength of your organization depends largely on your theatre classes. Even if you have a strong after-school attendance for auditions, rehearsals, drama club, or tournaments, your foundation is in your beginning drama classes. For starters, that is where you will find much of your outstanding talent. In addition, they are your audiences for your shows. And lastly, from this group will spring your advanced students for your higher-level drama classes.

Remember, theatre is an elective. It is imperative that your classes are filled to the brim with enticing activities that tempt even the shiest student to join. If your classes are fun, word of mouth from those who have witnessed your energetic lessons first-hand will ensure that you get some new students. If they are educational, teachers and administrators will recommend your classes, counselors will encourage students to take them, and parents will demand that their future lawyers and CEOs sign up. But there is still more that you can do.

> One year, my class was left out of the class selection catalog by mistake. I had to scramble to get my number out there to the students, not just at my campus, but at the feeders, too. Despite the error, I set a record with the number of new enrollees. They had to hire a second teacher to help with the class load!
>
> Suzi Zimmerman, Author

- First, advertise. Yes, offer an after-school drama party about a week before class selection for the next year. At this party, play plenty of games with attendees, and request students who are presently in your class to speak about the program. Make sure everyone knows your class number before leaving (the one students need to write on their class selection form).
- Take lots of pictures of students playing games and having fun in your classes, and then ask their permission (and their parents, too) to use the photos to promote your classes. Drop the pictures into posters with your class number and place them around school.
- There are many other ways to promote your program, too. Don't limit yourself to two or three. In marketing, saturation is the key. Try some of these strategies:
  - ~ Make announcements about your program over the school's PA system.
  - ~ Send personalized invitations to students who have attended your auditions and drama club meetings but are not in your classes; personally invite outstanding students in Drama One to audition for your most advanced class. Students and their parents appreciate hand-written, personal invitations.
  - ~ Ask the feeder schools if you and your top students can come talk about the program; involve them in some fun, easy games, but talk about the educational benefits, too.

Improv and Mime Troupes

Create an improvisation or mime troupe. Both can be wonderful additions to your existing organization, and they can even save you a great deal of time and money. In the end, you will see your club's bank account grow and your enrollment increase. Participants will gain the added benefit of being able to add an impressive item to their educational and professional resumes.

There are a number of ways having an improv or mime troupe can save your organization money:

- Unlike plays, you do not have to pay royalties for performing either of these.
- Rather than buying costumes, students can wear street clothes or company shirts with jeans for improvisation; for mime, they can purchase inexpensive costume pieces that can be used long-term.
- There are no scripts to buy.

And there are also a number of ways that both types of troupes will make you money:

- Produce a night of improvs instead of a show *or* in addition to your existing shows.
- Host improvisation competitions with several events and invite area schools to participate.
- Host improv and mime clinics for the younger students in your area and have your students teach the basics.
- Hook your company up with local gigs. A *gig* is a performance assignment, and depending on the length of time you spend, the number of actors you take, and so on, gigs can benefit you both financially and with added performance experience. Places to consider are children's hospitals, nursing facilities, public libraries, and business and charity organizations like the Lion's Club, the Rotary Club, and the Chamber of Commerce.

And, of course, there are a number of ways your troupe can gain exposure volunteering their talents and abilities. Both types of troupes can also serve as outreach organizations by providing young people in your area with a safe and healthy alternative to other less constructive leisure activities.

Improv and Mime Clinics, Workshops, and Camps

Host improv and mime educational activities for your feeder schools. Feeder schools are schools at the grades lower than yours that will eventually end up at your campus. For example, if you are currently at a middle school, your feeder schools are the elementaries that will generate your future students.

As you have already learned, reaching students before they select their classes is vital to your program's growth and survival. Unless these students and their parents understand what your program has to offer, they will not sign up for your classes. Reaching them about a year before they move to your school is a great way to build your program, and by charging for the activity, especially in the summer when young people become bored (and their parents become desperate), you have a wonderful source of revenue.

A *clinic* is a short but intense lesson in which the teacher works with students on a number of aspects. For example, your class might attend a clinic at an area university in which the professor works with a large group for an intense hour of targeted voice work or play polishing. The focus is on learning as much as you can in as short a time period as possible. Get an idea as to how your group can profit by looking at the sample clinic schedule and fees (figure 9C) that follows.

Workshops are a little different in that they are usually less intense and more enjoyable. Many workshops will have sessions so that those who attend may select the classes they want or need. Often, teachers and students learn side by side, and this is a wonderful opportunity to allow your students to become teachers. Furthermore, you can also seek out volunteer guest lecturers, keynote speakers, and performers. Sometimes these types of workshops precede competitions, so you may want to consider doing both back to back. See the sample workshop schedule and fees (figure 9A) to get an idea of how this works.

Camps are the most involved of these educational events. They may last for several days or even weeks, and in some cases, students stay overnight. However, most acting camps are day camps in which students attend for a half day (three to four hours) or a whole day (six to ten hours). The schedule is arranged so that students can expect to do the same basic classes each day, but the material offered within the structure changes and builds, culminating in a performance. Consider the sample camp schedule and fees (figure 9B) to see how a camp might work for you.

Sample Improvisation Workshop
Pike's Landing High School Theatre invites you to Acting Works, a series of workshops for young actors on July 6, 10 AM to 6 PM.

Session 1 – 10:00 AM to 11:30 AM
    Improvisation, Room 202
    Acting from the Feet Up, Room 208
    Costume fashion show by Costumes Galore, Main Stage
Session 2 – 11:45 AM to 1:15 PM
    Improvisation, Room 202
    Acting from the Feet Up, Room 208
    Starting an Improv Troupe at Your School, Main Stage
Lunch break – 1:15 PM to 2:45 PM (Palacial Pizza will sell pizza in the courtyard; Hot Diggity will sell hot dogs and sandwiches)
Session 3 – 2:45 PM to 4:15 PM
    Mime Your Own Business, Room 202
    Get Moving, Room 208
    Guest speaker, Babs McVee of McVee Talent Agency, Main Stage
Session 4 – 4:30 PM to 6:00 PM
    Mime Your Own Business, Room 202
    Promoting Your Theatre Program, Room 208
    Performance – an original improvisation show by the award-winning Pike's Landing HS Players

All actors, ages 10 and up, and their parents and teachers may attend. Sessions are $15 each, or all four for $50. Space is limited, so reserve your tickets today. More classes for each session may be available at time of workshops. If you are interested in teaching a workshop in exchange for a full-day ticket, contact Becky Hason at 972-555-5555.

(By limiting each small classroom to 30 students and by allowing 60 or more at the main stage, this group will make about $3000 for one day of work. They can make more by adding options to each session or by adding sessions. This idea works great when parents with theatre backgrounds volunteer to help or when area professionals donate their time and talents.)

(Figure 9A)

Sample Summer Day Camp

Theatre Off the Wall is hosting its annual summer day camp for ages 9 to 15 at Our Lady of the Lake Catholic Church on Broadway. The day camp is afternoons only, Monday through Friday, from June 6th through the 17th. All campers will receive an official Rotten Tomatoes T-shirt and a daily snack. On the final day, June 17, family and friends are invited to attend The Rotten Tomatoes Showcase from 7 to 9 PM (admission free for parents, $3 for siblings and friends).

Daily schedule:
1:00 – 1:30 Campers arrive
1:30 – 2:00 Improvisation games – all participate!
2:00 – 3:00 Mime and pantomime
3:00 – 3:15 Snack time (will be provided)
3:15 – 3:30 Rotten Tomato showcase
        (campers will watch video of prior camp showcases)
3:30 – 4:00 Acting basics
4:00 – 5:00 Intensive improvisation
5:00 – 5:30 Campers depart

Dates to remember:
June 6 – First day of camp; teams selected
June 8 – Team captains selected
June 10 – Awards for week one
June 13 – Special guest teacher, Roger Mayhery from University
        of Southlake theatre
June 14 – Picture day, look nice!
June 17 – Awards for week two; bring your T-shirts (but don't
        wear them); no parent pick up at 5:00; see you at 7PM
        for the showcase.

Limited to first forty enrollees — $125 for two-week session. There are a limited number of spots for camp counselors with high school acting experience (must be in 11th or 12th grade).

Contact Brent King at 214-555-5555 for more information.

(Figure 9B)

Sample Mime Clinic

Rogers High School Mime Troupe, *Sh!*, invites you to a mime clinic on July 6, 10 AM to 8 PM.

- Each clinic is one hour and class size is limited to 35. Smaller visiting groups may be combined by the facilitator or program planner, but they will not exceed the limit.
- Individuals and parents are welcomed to attend and participate, but all must be registered.
- All classes are taught by a member of the Rogers High School Mime Group *"Sh!"* A parent will supervise all sessions.
- The clinic is $10 per person; groups of 10 or more are $8 per person. You may reserve a private room for $245. This is a savings of $105 for a group of 35!

(In a best-case scenario, this school may make as much as $3500 in a day for each session of students paying $10 each. Two simultaneous sessions will make $7000, and three will make $10,500. Realistically speaking, if this were an actual clinic, it is doubtful all sessions would be filled. A great deal depends on the size of the town, the amount of publicity, and the reputation of the troupe. They could reduce the numbers in each class, start small, and build. Regardless, this is a great way to increase any program's exposure and build a club's revenue.)

(Figure 9C)

Drama Club

Do you have a drama club? It is effortless, and it might just be your best resource for talent.

For the eager learner, there are never enough hours in the day to take all the classes offered at a school. It could be that your class is desired by many who cannot fit it into their schedules. By offering a time after school for enrichment activities in theatre (and, of course, to manage the business of the program), you are opening another slot in busy kids' days.

For the actors in your class, they may not feel as comfortable giving their performances 100 percent if they think the others in their same period are not fully dedicated. However, in drama club, with actors they feel are there for the same reasons they are, the atmospshere lends itself to giving it everything they've got. You may discover that a young person you had originally thought was, well — okay — is really very talented! She just needed the comfort and freedom of being a part of the club.

Within this organized club, you will find it easier to form an improv or mime troupe. Even if you choose not to have a full-fledged company of spontaneous performers, you can include mime and improv as a part of the meetings. Many clubs use a section of games as the focus of their meetings. For example, for a one-hour meeting, take care of business for the first half-hour, and end with an additional half-hour of educational and fun improv games. No one will strongly desire attending your club meetings for the business alone, but it is necessary. However, rewarding the club with games after addressing the business items will win your organization many fans. It is a single brick in a strong foundation.

Perform for Area PTAs

Parent Teacher Associations and Parent Teacher Student Organizations (PTAs and PTSOs) are wonderful audiences for educational performing groups. They are usually happy to have choirs and drama troupes perform for them. Savvy teachers seek audiences with both their own schools and their feeder schools' organizations. Because of the make-up of their audiences, these are ideal marketing outlets for you. Remember to keep it short and sweet, leave them wanting more, and boast the educational benefits.

There are a number of games that are either conducive to audience participation or are at least very entertaining to an audience. These are the activities you want to capitalize on when doing an improv show. (See list on the following page.)

Start by asking all or part of the audience to complete a quick survey (title yours to match your program's name) like the Tomato Farmer's Pick (see figure 9D). This form, used by the Rotten Tomatoes, will help the players

Tomato Farmer's Pick

List three words to describe any superhero:

_____ _____ _____

What are some events where people tend to "say the wrong thing"?

_____

_____

_____

List three professions or occupations; circle yours. _____ _____ _____

What is your name? _____

(Figure 9D)

209

with three of their games: *Superheroes, World's Worst Things to Say,* and *Old Job, New Job.* Lastly, by having the audience member write his name, you can mention him when you use his suggestions. This makes your audience feel involved. Also, after demonstrating a game, the players can then select a player from the audience and play again. Audience participation is a wonderful way to make your event memorable.

You can customize your audience survey form to fit the games you intend to play. Completing the form should not take any of your stage time and can be done by volunteerism as your audience enters.

Let students do all of the talking. The parents will be impressed more by your students' enthusiasm for your program than by your own. Furthermore, because theatre is not where many parents hope their young people will venture, allowing students to speak reminds parents that drama class will also prepare them to become outstanding orators.

Plan on about three activities, but keep an eye on the time. Your goal is to promote your program, and running even a few minutes over can look really bad. Also, remind your young people how important appropriateness is. While it is always imperative that we teach our actors to find humor in the truly funny rather than in embarrassment and bathroom humor, it will be even more important in front of the parents of your future and present students.

Suggested Activities for Improvisation Performances
17. Sit, Stand, and Bend
23. I Am!
31. The Backwards Selling Game
36. Touch On/Touch Off
37. World's Worst Things to Say
38. The ABC Game
39. The Question Game
42. The Dating Game
49. Key Words
53. Dubbing
54. Party Crashers
55. Whose Line Is Next?
56. Movie Styles
57. George Is Late Again!
58. Old Job, New Job
59. The Beauty Experiment

60. Superheroes
62. Mannequins
65. Murder Mystery
73. Expert Olympics
75. What Are You Doing? (works best in limited, short rounds; experiment with using audience volunteers)
77. Pantomime Race (break your audience into teams, too, and let them root for their side)

Teach Teachers to Use Games in Their Classrooms

There are many teachers both outside and inside theatre who recognize the benefits of having fun and using compelling lessons, but they don't know how or where to begin. You and your students can host a "Teaching with Games" workshop for them. In many districts, additional hours of teacher learning such as this are required. For this reason, you may be able to get funding from your district for things like making photocopies and transparencies and providing your attendees with packets.

Start by narrowing your activities down to as many as you feel you can teach within the time frame you have been given (or within the time you will request). Remember to allow several minutes to play the games or activities with the teachers. Like your students, they, too, will learn better by doing. Also keep in mind that you should select activities that will benefit teachers (and eventually their students) from other curriculums. Next, create a packet telling how to play each game and specifying how it applies to various classes. Leave plenty of room in your packets for notes. Next, get ready to teach. You and your students will demonstrate the games and activities, and then you can break into groups (allow a student to head each group) and let the teachers play.

This is not a huge money-making endeavor for your program, but it will be a super tool for promoting your program and its reputation. There are not many opportunities for a drama teacher to share what she does with her fellow teachers other than having them come see her shows. This is a way to share your program, allow your students to become teachers, and to show teachers within your school that learning can take place in a fun environment.

Host an Improv and/or Mime Competition

If making money for your program is your main objective, consider hosting an improvisation competition. Like the workshops and clinics mentioned earlier, this can be done in your school on a single weekend day with minimal up-front expense and planning. Furthermore, it can be done in conjunction with or as a follow-up to the clinics and workshops.

- Start by soliciting parent volunteers
- Decide how you want to divide your competition
  - ~ Age groups
  - ~ Activities
  - ~ Rounds
- Decide how winners will be awarded
  - ~ Prizes for top 10, 5, or 3
  - ~ Everyone is given a score or rank (Superior, Excellent, or Good)
  - ~ A combination of the above two suggestions
- Decide how judging will be conducted
  - ~ Student judges from your school
  - ~ Student judges from a higher-level school
  - ~ Paid judges
  - ~ Parent volunteers
- Consider the following:
  - ~ On which categories will actors be judged at each level?
  - ~ What activities will students demonstrate in their competitions?
  - ~ Will you have some group activities where teams compete together?
  - ~ What will you give as prizes (trophies, ribbons, etc.)?
  - ~ How much will you charge?
  - ~ Where will you hold the competition?
  - ~ How many simultaneous rounds will you have?
  - ~ Will your students teach classes prior to hosting the competition?
  - ~ Will there be a showcase afterward?

There are a number of factors to consider when hosting a competition. Because it can become overwhelming, start with only one age group, a few activities, and a few awards. After you feel this is under control and easily managed, add another age group or break the competition into preliminaries and finals. If you become competent with a simple competition and build on that in future years, you will create a reputation for your program that will promote greater attendance. However, if you try to do too much too soon, you will hurt your program's reputation. Keep it simple, and after your roots are firmly established, you can grow.

Helpful Starters

Sometimes getting started can be the hardest part of performing a creative improvisation. The following categories are suggestions that can spark a new level of performance in your classroom. When you need a multifaceted character, try taking one item from each category. For example, if you took the first word from each group, instead of a lawyer, you would have an aging lawyer who is locked out of his car at the beach.

Characteristics:

Aging	Body-building	Loud-mouthed	Cannot stop talking
Tired	In slow motion	Fast-talking	Cannot stop laughing
Joyful	Air-headed	Hyperactive	Cannot stop crying
Sexy	Country	Religious/holy	Cannot stop snorting
Childish	Hot-headed	Complimentary	Cannot stop staring
Flirting	Exaggerating	Bad-breathed	Cannot stop lying
Bossy	Mind-changing	Negotiating	Cannot stop hiccupping
Timid	Shoplifting	Whining	Cannot stay awake
Cold	Sneezing	Eavesdropping	Cannot see clearly
Queasy	Concerned	Apologetic	Cannot hear clearly

Characters:

Lawyer	Hypochondriac	Person with a split personality
Policeman	Crocodile hunter	Kindly kindergarten teacher
Teacher	TV talk show host	Bride/groom late for wedding
Southern belle	Auctioneer	Someone who makes lists
Old man/woman	Ballerina	Aerobics instructor
Witch doctor	Investigator	Sorority sister
Superhero	Salesman	Surfer dude
Rodeo clown	Tightrope walker	Psychic
Hillbilly	Preacher	Action film movie star
Snob	Actress/actor	Astronaut
Pirate	Mime	Special agent on a mission
Broadway dancer	Psychiatrist	Someone hearing voices
Doctor	Child	Angel
Dentist		

Situations: One of the characters ...

Is locked out of his/her car	Is kidnapping the other
Wakes from sleepwalking	Is applying for a job
Is about to bungee jump	Is robbing the other
Is doing research at a library	Is always changing the subject
Is meeting the fiancé's parents	Is extremely forgetful
Has three wishes	Has a very annoying habit
Is asking the other for directions	Is seeking advice from a psychic

Is a double agent, spying on the other
Is awarding other with sweepstake grand prize
Is asking the other for his/her hand in marriage
Cannot bring him/herself to say something
Thinks he/she is really attractive, smart, etc.
Is trying to teach the other how to dance, sing, etc.

Settings:

At the beach	In an airplane
Between takes on a movie set	At the mall
In a beauty parlor	While attempting to play in a symphony
In an elevator	In math class
In the Tunnel of Love	At a playground
In a wind storm	While escaping from prison
In a car	In an operating room
On the front porch	In the nursery
While trying not to be noticed	At the library
In yoga class	While fighting off a wild beast
At the police station	On a roller coaster
While playing video games	At a pie-eating contest
In the middle of a robbery	In the middle of a Wild West shootout
At one character's wedding	While on stage opening night of a play

While conducting traffic at a busy intersection
While posing for a big fashion layout

The following examples of how the characteristics, characters, situations, and settings can be randomly combined will help you to see how they can benefit your improvisation:

- A body-building, hypochondriac TV talk show host is seeking advice from a psychic in math class
- A religious/holy, Southern belle cannot stop talking while asking the other actor for directions while escaping from prison

- An air-headed crocodile hunter cannot stop snorting while conducting busy intersection traffic and making his three wishes
- A loud-mouthed, sexy policeman is a double agent, spying on the other actor at the playground
- A slow-motion psychiatrist cannot stop crying and cannot bring him/herself to say something to the other actor in an elevator
- A joyful, country teacher in a wind storm is meeting his/her fiancé's parents
- A tired, fast-talking person with a split personality is awarding the other actor with a sweepstake grand prize

Glossary of Target Areas

The following descriptions will assist you in understanding the target areas listed before each game and in the index.

Awareness – Being aware of everything going on around you when in a scene is not being unfocused. That is, unless you allow your awareness to interfere with your performance. Rather, being aware simply means knowing more about the scene than just what you bring into it. Actors who are aware usually end up covering for actors who are not and who eventually make a mistake because of their self-centeredness.

Breathing Control – Breathing is involuntary, but breathing incorrectly is not. Some actors let their breathing control them, but those who use proper breathing can manipulate it, use it to their advantage, and they do not find themselves breathless at the end of a long monolog (unless, of course, their character is out of breath!). Like singers, actors must learn to breathe properly, and then they must practice.

Character – The ability to explore characterization fully can separate a good actor from a great one. These activities offer the opportunity to learn and practice this skill.

Confidence – Many of the students in your class like performing, but they lack the confidence to really open up in front of their peers. Oftentimes, theatre teachers start with giant steps, assigning the class a monolog or duet. Some students love the challenge, but for others, they see nothing in their performance futures but failure, so they don't even try. Instead of alienating your shier, more reluctant learners, start with baby steps. Activities under "Confidence" will have these kids performing energetically before they even realize it.

Creative Thinking – Thinking "outside the box," while cliché, is the best way to define creative thinking.

Dramatic Structure – The structure of a drama (of any story) is basically the same: It must have a beginning or exposition, some sort of conflict or obstacle, rising action, a climax, and an ending. Some of the activities listed will help students to identify the structure of a scene and others will assist them in creating a scene with a solid dramatic structure.

Dressing the Stage – Just as you carefully arrange the flowers in a spring bouquet so that they make a pretty display, the characters and setting on stage must be arranged to create focus and energy. Dressing the stage allows actors to explore sharing the stage, shifting focus, using levels, and practice not upstaging one another.

Energy – When a scene is energetic, it is dynamic. This simply means that the message never lilts or fails to be expressed, even in silence. Energy does not necessarily mean movement, and it certainly does not mean yelling and running. A character can be energetic while standing perfectly still and while remaining silent. Energy is somewhat intangible, but it is obvious when it is present and sorely missed when it is absent.

Eye Contact/Nonverbals – Eye contact and nonverbal communication are the foundation of expression. "The eyes are the window to the soul," but when the eyes are flitting back and forth, breaking the fourth wall, or seeking the director's approval, the window is slammed shut. As with instincts, eye contact and nonverbal communication in a scene should represent the character, not the actor.

Facial Expressions – As with movement, actors on stage will often stop portraying emotions naturally out of fear. Young actors may fear what their peers will think if they show their emotions, because showing emotion makes humans vulnerable. Activities listed under "Facial Expressions" will help actors to become comfortable with bringing their emotions to the surface and allowing others to see them.

Focus – Synonymous with concentration, focus is when actors stay in the moment. Anything that is not a part of a scene is tuned out.

Following Directions – Of course, actors must be able to take direction, so many of these games challenge them with difficult directions.

Getting to Know You – These activities allow students to learn about one another, promoting the "theatre family" atmosphere needed to become truly relaxed in front of one another.

Imagery and Recall – Actors who use observation as a form of filing away mental images for future use will benefit from and excel at these activities, which force actors to remember images and then to express details about them to their audience

Instincts – Instincts are feelings. They are difficult to define, they are not very tangible, and they are often the first thing we fail to use when they are needed most. Actors must develop good instincts, but often, they will be the thing called into question during rehearsals. An actor will try something new because he felt like it. If the director questions his motivation and the actor simply replies that he felt like it, the director will likely not buy it. The reason is, the actor may have felt like it, but would the character have felt like it? If so, why would the character have felt like it? It's the answer to the question "Why?" that will sell the director on the idea. Actors must develop instincts, but then they must be able to recognize how various characters would respond to them.

Learning Information – These activities will help students learn new vocabulary, theatre history facts, or other information-intensive subjects.

Listening – Like being aware, listening (especially in improvisation) means attending to more of the scene than just what you bring into it. Actors who do not listen in improvisation get "lost." They do not know how to respond to what their co-actors say because they do not really hear it.

Movement – Because we move freely throughout the day every day, it is something that beginning actors assume will just happen on stage. However, when the audience is watching, when we are not ourselves but another character, free movement seems elusive. Many new actors report feeling naked on stage, so they don't move, because that would draw attention to their nakedness. The truth is, the feeling they are experiencing is called vulnerability, and like frightened animals, young, inexperienced actors freeze so that they will not draw attention to themselves. Studying movement not only allows actors to shake the vulnerable feeling, it teaches them to understand and manipulate their bodies so that they can better express themselves.

Pantomime – Pantomime is the act of pretending to do something but not really doing it. For example, one might pretend to open a door without using a door prop. You will find an entire chapter on pantomime, and many of the activities in the other chapters will also include pantomime-building skills.

Presentation – This is the overall package, the production. These activities will allow actors to create an enjoyable entertainment experience for their eager audiences.

Relaxation – Being relaxed on stage is the same as being comfortable. Relaxed actors feel freedom to express without holding back. They can move without being afraid of looking funny. They may experience some stage fright, but to them, it is welcomed adrenaline, not a debilitating fear.

Self-Control – As plays are rehearsed, actors learn to trust their fellow actors because they develop routines during the weeks preceding a show. However, there are times when something instigates "the unexpected" on stage. By maintaining self-control during unexpected situations like these, the situation can be quickly resolved without ever detracting from the message. Self-control is also vital when doing group work, stage combat, stage kisses, or other highly emotional moments and special effects.

Stage Combat – None of these scenes will teach your students stage combat. Like ballet, it must be taught by a trained professional or someone will get hurt. However, some of these games will allow your students to practice it only if they have learned it already. Remind students that wrestling moves are not acceptable in improvisation or pantomime.

Stage Fright – Stage fright is fear of performing in front of an audience. It may stem from a lack of confidence, but even seasoned, award-winning actors may still get stage fright occasionally. The best cures for stage fright are learning to relax and developing a "relationship" with the stage. These activities will assist your young actors with becoming relaxed and comfortable on the stage and in front of an audience.

Strategic Thinking – If creative thinking is thinking "outside the box," then strategic thinking is taking the box apart and putting it back together again to better suit your needs. Strategic thinkers solve problems and improve processes.

Teamwork – Actors and crews who work together on projects become extremely close, like families or teams. It is important that they be able to work toward common goals in a friendly and professional manner. Activities under "Teamwork" will promote this among your actors.

Timing – One of the most difficult acting elements to master, timing is the ability to judge and then react appropriately to the rhythm and pace of a scene. Often, timing is instinctual, meaning actors — after learning all they can about the events involved — react with their feelings and gut reactions about how the characters would pace themselves. Many clues can be found in scripts, but in improvisation, the clues are in the situation.

Trust – Because acting teams are so close and depend on each other so much, trust is very important. Actors must trust that their fellow actors will not spring surprises on them in the middle of a performance, and the light guy must trust that the actor will find his way to a mark before he brings up a pin spot. Most of the activities in theatre and in this book are based on this simple concept. It is important that everyone remembers it works two ways — you earn it, and you practice it.

Voice – Almost any speaking activity will allow actors not just to use their voices, but to train them. Things to consider when improving one's voice include *pace* (not speaking too fast, or in some cases too slowly), *clarity* (articulation and diction), and volume. Actors also need to be able to manipulate their *pitch* (how high or low one's voice is) and their *expression* (the ability to get a message across), and it is helpful to be able to use unique vocal characterizations and accents.

Target Areas Index

Use this index to find games to specifically target areas where your group is experiencing difficulty, or you can format your lesson plan and syllabus around a weekly or daily activity to suit the unit of study. Each activity has been listed under its target areas so that you can quickly find one that fits your needs. See Appendix B for an explanation of the target areas.

Resources

For more information on teaching your students the basics of acting and improvisation, check out some of these books from Meriwether Publishing Ltd.:

Theatre Games for Young Performers by Maria Novelly
Group Improvisation by Peter Gwinn (with contributions from Charna Halpern)
Theatre Games and Beyond by Amiel Schotz
The Ultimate Improv Book by Edward J. Nevraumont and Nicholas P. Hanson (with contributions from Kurt Smeaton)
Truth in Comedy by Charna Halpern, Del Close, and Kim "Howard" Johnson
Improvisation for Actors and Writers by Bill Lynn
Spontaneous Performance by Marsh Cassady
Comedy Improvisation by Delton T. Horn
Acting Games — Improvisations and Exercises by Marsh Cassady
Improvisations in Creative Drama by Betty Keller
Improve with Improv! by Brie Jones

You can also learn more about basic acting terminology and getting started in improvisation by exploring these fun improvisation web sites. (Remember that web sites can change without warning. At the time this book was published, the suggested sites were completely appropriate for all ages. As always, use care and discretion when allowing your students to surf the Internet.)

www.creativedrama.com
www.fuzzyco.com
www.byu.edu/tma/arts-ed
www.svsu.edu/theatre/summercamps/theatregames.htm
www.improv.ca/ — The official web site for The Canadian Improv Games

About the Author

Suzi Zimmerman is a veteran of the stage. After competing in pageants and talent competitions from an early age and winning many state and national competitions, it became apparent that show business was in her future. She attended Kilgore College, home of the Texas Shakespeare Festival, on an acting scholarship and continued her education at Texas A&M University in Commerce, Texas. She founded Theatre Off the Wall, a small acting company, and has been instrumental in developing a number of additional theatre programs. She is a professional actor and voice artist for commercials and educational videos. On top of that, she is a full-time public school educator, teaches private lessons, and conducts group workshops, all on the subject of theatre.

Order Form

Meriwether Publishing Ltd.
PO Box 7710
Colorado Springs CO 80933-7710
Phone: 800-937-5297 Fax: 719-594-9916
Website: www.meriwether.com

Please send me the following books:

_____ **More Theatre Games for**   **$17.95**
Young Performers #BK-B268
by Suzi Zimmerman
Improvisations and exercises for developing acting skills

_____ **Theatre Games for Young Performers**   **$16.95**
#BK-B188
by Maria C. Novelly
Improvisations and exercises for developing acting skills

_____ **Acting Games — Improvisations and**   **$16.95**
Exercises #BK-B168
by Marsh Cassady
A textbook of theatre games and improvisations

_____ **Theatre Games and Beyond #BK-B217**   **$17.95**
by Amiel Schotz
A creative approach for performers

_____ **Improve with Improv! #BK-B160**   **$14.95**
by Brie Jones
A guide to improvisation and character development

_____ **Group Improvisation #BK-B259**   **$15.95**
by Peter Gwinn with additional material by Charna Halpern
The manual of ensemble improv games

_____ **The Ultimate Improv Book #BK-B248**   **$17.95**
by Edward J. Nevraumont, Nicholas P. Hanson and Kurt Smeaton
A complete guide to comedy improvisation

These and other fine Meriwether Publishing books are available at
your local bookstore or direct from the publisher. Prices subject to
change without notice. Check our website or call for current prices.

Name: _____ e-mail: _____

Organization name: _____

Address: _____

City: _____ State: _____

Zip: _____ Phone: _____

❑ **Check enclosed**

❑ **Visa / MasterCard / Discover #** _____

Signature: _____ *Expiration date:* _____
              (required for credit card orders)

Colorado residents: Please add 3% sales tax.
Shipping: Include $3.95 for the first book and 75¢ for each additional book ordered.

❑ *Please send me a copy of your complete catalog of books and plays.*